The Marriage Challenge is an ... in their finances. The story fo... the husband and wife. God has designed your marriage to showcase the gospel. Don't let financial issues get in the way of a great marriage. Read *The Marriage Challenge*!

Daniel L. Akin, president of Southeastern Baptist
Theological Seminary, Wake Forest, North Carolina

I have known and worked with Art Rainer for several years and have always been encouraged by his infectious, 360-degree vision for mission in every part of life. This fuels his works on careful thinking and management of money—from personal devotion to marriage, from raising kids to leadership, the local church, education, and understanding the world. I am pleased to recommend this to you.

Keith and Kristyn Getty, modern hymn writers,
authors of *Sing!: How Worship Transforms Your Life, Family, and Church*

Art Rainer is the new voice in personal finance for Christians. His writings and podcasts are awakening believers to grasp more completely God's plan for the money He has entrusted to us. His latest book, *The Marriage Challenge*, is an incredible resource for all married couples from engaged couples to newlyweds to those married for many years. Get it and apply its principles immediately!

Thom S. Rainer, president of LifeWay Christian Resources

The Marriage Challenge is a must-read for married couples. The book is crafted in such a way that is entertaining, biblically sound, and practical. I wish that I had this book during my first few years of marriage. To be honest, I'm glad I have it now!

Jimmy Scroggins, senior pastor of Family Church,
West Palm Beach, Florida

Whether you are newly married or have been married for years, this book is for you! Art provides clear, practical steps toward financial health, and addresses underlying issues couples experience that present themselves in their finances. Both your marriage and your bank account will be stronger by applying the principles found in this book! Art Rainer's writing style is like having your own personal marriage and financial counselor and advisor. His personal and often entertaining approach helps to break down barriers for couples creating the opportunity for greater unity and success in their approach to money. This book is guaranteed to positively impact the reader!

Selma Wilson, senior vice president of LifeWay Christian Resources

Love, money, and the pursuit of happiness. Unfortunately, for too many couples, money and happiness never go hand-in-hand. In fact, I find money as one of the single biggest reasons for emotional disconnection in marriage. Not only does Art provide an incredibly succinct, practical framework for married couples to plan financially, he also covers the relational dynamics necessary for becoming one in money and marriage! I will now recommend this book to every pre-marital couple I work with.

Josh Straub, author of *Safe House* and host of the *In This Together* podcast

I would have never thought I'd be on the edge of my seat reading a book about finances and marriage. Art's ability to tell a story kept me turning the pages and his practical advice had me readily thinking about what steps my husband and I could apply to our marriage. This is a book for any couple who wants to honor God with their finances while growing closer together.

Julie Masson, columnist for *Parenting Teens*

Praise for *The Money Challenge*

Art has written an incredibly practical, readable, useful book on living openhandedly with our finances. *The Money Challenge* offers practical steps to live as God has designed us to: as channels of His great generosity, to advance His Kingdom. I highly recommend it!

Matt Carter, pastor of preaching and vision,
The Austin Stone Community Church, Austin, Texas

I can't wait for you to read Art's book. It is so good. Art encourages and equips you in *The Money Challenge*. Not only will you learn a lot, but you will also enjoy his captivating writing style.

Derwin L. Gray, lead pastor, Transformation Church,
Indian Land, South Carolina

Sometimes the hardest part of wise financial stewardship is knowing where to start. That's where Art's book comes in—his relatable stories and practical steps break down a seemingly impossible goal to simple, faith-filled steps. Join him in this thirty-day challenge and watch as God uses this book to propel you into a lifestyle of generous giving. Around The Summit Church we always say, "Live sufficiently, give extravagantly." This is how to start.

J.D. Greear, PhD, pastor of The Summit Church,
Raleigh-Durham, North Carolina, and author,
Gaining by Losing: Why the Future Belongs to Churches that Send

The Money Challenge is a hopeful, gospel-oriented primer on using finances for the sake of the Kingdom. Everyone can benefit from the biblical wisdom here, regardless of financial or social background.

Russell Moore, president, Southern Baptist
Ethics & Religious Liberty Commission

Who knew generosity was such a driving force for how we handle our money in a God-honoring way? Art Rainer helps us understand why in this helpful book, *The Money Challenge*. If we're honest, money is one of the hardest topics for us to face and tackle in our hearts and minds. That is one of many reasons we are served by Rainer's work here. Practical, wise, and challenging, you'll be glad you picked up this helpful book.

Trillia Newbell, author of *Enjoy, Fear and Faith,* and *United*

THE
MARRIAGE
CHALLENGE

A FINANCE GUIDE FOR MARRIED COUPLES

ART RAINER

PUBLISHING GROUP

NASHVILLE, TENNESSEE

978-1-5359-1238-9

Published by B&H Publishing Group
Nashville, Tennessee

Dewey Decimal Classification: 332.024
Subject Heading: PERSONAL FINANCE
\ MONEY \ MARRIAGE

Cover design and illustration by Darren Welch.
Additional illustration ©shutterstock/Serhiy
Smirnov. Photo ©123rf.com/rangizzz.

1 2 3 4 5 6 7 • 22 21 20 19 18

For Sarah

Acknowledgments

I am grateful for everyone who made this book possible. I feel truly blessed to have been given such a great opportunity with such great support.

Given that the topic of this book centers on money and marriage, it should not surprise anyone that I first want to thank my wife, Sarah. She is an amazingly godly, smart, and courageous wife and mom. Thank you for your love and inspiration.

I am grateful for the three boys God has given me. They bring a lot of fun, energy, and clogged toilets to our house. To Nathaniel, Joshua, and James—I love you. I am proud of you. And I am glad that you are my sons.

The rest of my family needs mentioning as well. They have provided continued support and encouragement over the years. Dad and Mom, thank you for providing a godly home in which to grow up. Sam, Jess, and your crews, I love you all.

The team at B&H Publishing is incredible. I am so thankful for their partnership on this project. Thank you, Devin Maddox, Taylor Combs, Dave Schroeder, and Jenaye White.

Southeastern Baptist Theological Seminary in Wake Forest, North Carolina, is an incredible community of Great Commission-focused believers. I consider it an honor to serve alongside such a wonderful team. Specifically, I want to thank Amy Whitfield and Mandy Bramlett for their involvement with this book. Your input was invaluable.

Of course, I am most grateful for my Lord and Savior Jesus Christ. My hope is that this book makes his name more famous.

Contents

xii   THE MARRIAGE CHALLENGE

DECIDE TO DESTROY MARRIAGE DIVIDERS

8 Money Milestones

Milestone 1: Start giving.

Milestone 2: Save $1,500 for a minor emergency.

Milestone 3: Max out your 401(k) or 403(b) match.

Milestone 4: Pay off all debt except your mortgage.

Milestone 5: Save three to six months of living
expenses for a job-loss emergency.

Milestone 6: Put 15 percent of your gross income to retirement.

Milestone 7: Save for college or pay off your mortgage.

Milestone 8: Live generously.

Palm Trees and Arguments

The yelling sharply contrasted with the rest of the scene.

Miami Beach was showing off. The sky was a perfect blue, and no cloud had made an appearance all day long. The beach's sand was a perfect tan, peppered with seashells. The sun's rays glistened on the blue ocean like a thousand tiny diamonds. They sparkled so brightly that one could only glance at them for a moment without squinting and turning to look elsewhere. And that was okay. There were plenty of beautiful, tropical views to enjoy.

It was the type of day that kept guests of The Miami Palm Resort and Spa returning for more. The seven-story white art deco-style building had become somewhat of a landmark for Miami Beach.

At the resort's entrance, new arrivals were greeted by a light, ocean breeze. They stepped out of their rental car and inhaled the salt air. The potted palm trees at the front steps greeted them with a slight sway. Welcome to paradise.

Everything seemed right.

Which is exactly why the yelling could not be missed. It was a complete contradiction of everything that should happen in that moment—relaxation, awe, and laughter.

But there stood Chris at the front of the building, right where guests were greeted, pacing back and forth, arguing vehemently with the person on the other side of the phone.

"Why didn't you tell me? You do realize that my company is considering layoffs right now? What if I lose my job? What then? We were already close to the financial edge. Now we are on it. I can't believe this!"

His motions had become somewhat predictable to the onlookers. When he spoke, his arm went in the air and his hand spread wide open. When he listened, he closed his eyes and pressed his hand tightly against his forehead. His facial expression communicated one thing— utter frustration.

Chris took a deep breath and tried to compose himself. "Look, I need to go for a walk. This is just not how I imagined the start of our marriage going down. I'll be back to the room in an hour or so. I just need to cool down."

He paused for a couple of seconds to listen. "Yes. Me too. Bye." And then he hung up.

Chris sighed out loud and looked to see a few guests and resort staff members uneasily eyeing him. He responded with an awkward tight-lipped smile and head nod. They went their way. Chris stood still.

"Mr. Chris, how is your and Mrs. Claire's honeymoon going?" It was the greeter at the front door. He was an elderly man, probably in his eighties. Chris figured that he was probably too old to take on any other positions at the resort. And at the same time he was pleasant. So a greeter role probably fit him well. He had only briefly spoken to the man when they first arrived, which is why Chris was surprised the man remembered his name.

"I'm impressed you remembered our names. I have to admit that I don't remember catching yours." Chris reached out to shake the greeter's hand.

"Most people around here call me Mr. Gunther. But I'll respond to 'excuse me' or 'hey' just the same. I'm here for you and all the resort guests. So however you want to get my attention is fine with me. But I will warn you that you must speak a little loud. This hearing aid isn't as good as advertised!"

Mr. Gunther grabbed Chris's hand and shook it. Chris chuckled lightly.

"Now that's what I like to see from guests of The Miami Palm Resort and Spa."

"How long have you worked here?" asked Chris.

"Oh, sixty years or so. I just can't seem to leave the place."

Chris's eyes became wide open, shocked at what he just heard. "Did you say sixty years?"

"I did. Time sure has flown. This has been a special place for me. Did you know that I met my wife, Rose, right over there at that desk?" He pointed at a wooden desk in the lobby where Chris and Claire had checked in the other day. "She was the receptionist. In my opinion, there hasn't been a prettier lady to work the desk since."

Chris paused, clearly in thought. "So, you've had a long marriage?"

"One that lasts a lifetime," Mr. Gunther said as he patted Chris on the back. "My sweet Rose passed away a few years back. There is not day that I don't think about her. It's one of the reasons why I love this place. It reminds me of her."

Chris smiled at his remarks. "Did you ever face any financial challenges?"

"Of course. Most of us have," replied Mr. Gunther.

"Well, do you have any advice for a newlywed?" responded Chris.

Mr. Gunther paused, clearly in thought.

"You know, maybe. Chris, I want this honeymoon to be special for you and Claire. Would you be open to hanging out with an old man and his friends while you're here?"

This was not something Chris would normally jump at. It definitely wasn't part of the original honeymoon plan. But the honeymoon had already veered way off course and into a ditch anyway, and he and Claire needed help getting out. Since Mr. Gunther offered, he might as well take him up on it. What could it hurt?

"Sure," responded Chris.

Decide to Be One

A financially healthy couple doesn't start with a checking account. It starts with unity. It starts with sacrificial, selfless love. It starts with both husband and wife moving away from "me" and toward "we." Through this the gospel is displayed, and true financial health can be pursued.

CHAPTER I
Oneness

Chris and Mr. Gunther walked around the building to the pool deck facing the beach. Chris assumed that it was okay for Mr. Gunther to leave his post at the front door. Mr. Gunther didn't hesitate, so Chris didn't either. What were they going to do, fire a man who had worked there for sixty years?

"Man, this is a beautiful place," said Chris as he looked out over the pool and beach.

Mr. Gunther smiled, the wrinkles on his face made it evident that smiling was his most frequent expression. "Chris, I couldn't help but overhear the conversation you were having with Claire. I hate hearing those types of arguments between newlyweds. Is everything okay?"

Chris smirked. "Did you really just bring me back here to get me away from the other guests?"

Mr. Gunther chuckled. "Well, no. But maybe I should have earlier! I just like the view back here."

Chris wasn't sure how much to tell Mr. Gunther. After all, he just met him. But he seemed genuine enough. "As you can tell, we had a pretty big argument earlier. What you heard was more of a follow-up argument. For some reason, Claire decided that now was the right time to reveal her credit card and student loan debt. She never said anything about it while we were dating or engaged. I can't believe she kept it from me."

"Hmm. I see," Mr. Gunther said with a look of concern. "And why does that bother you?

Chris was a little taken aback by the question. The answer seemed apparent. "Well, obviously, there's the trust issue. And second, now we have this deep financial pit that we have to get out of. I have no idea how we can do it. And as if that weren't enough, my company is in the middle of layoffs. I have no idea whether or not my job will be cut. I had this dream of being young and financially healthy, making a mark on this world, and now we're just young, in debt, and potentially jobless."

Mr. Gunther put his hands in his pockets. "Well, there's a lot to unpack there. It's funny, Rose and I weren't too different from you and Claire when we first got married. Granted, neither one of us had a lot of debt, but we were broke. And, boy, did we have some arguments about money. Some were brutal. The financial stress seemed to get the best of both of us."

Chris replied, "From what I hear, money tends to be a pretty big issue in marriage. My older brother got a divorce last year because of money issues. Already having arguments about money makes me wonder if Claire and I will make it. And I hate that thought."

"Well, you don't want that, do you?"

"Of course not. I didn't marry Claire only to get a divorce. But what scares me is that my brother didn't marry his wife thinking that they would get a divorce either. But money got in the way."

Mr. Gunther looked out toward the ocean and was quiet for a few seconds. Then he spoke, as if to himself. "Contentment and purpose."

"Excuse me?" questioned Chris.

"Contentment and purpose. It's what changed our marriage and money issues. You see, God has a design for our marriage and our money. When we chase that design, we find ourselves content and purposeful. When we move away from it, we find ourselves dissatisfied and lost."

Chris's head was nodding in agreement, but he wasn't sure how to respond. "Okay. So, I guess the next question is, how?"

Mr. Gunther pulled his hands from his pockets and crossed his arms. "Oneness. It starts there," Mr. Gunther said with confidence.

"What do you mean?"

"Our resort has received a number of awards over the years. The ones on which we pride ourselves most are the ones that deal with customer experience."

Chris knew this. It was one of the reasons they chose The Miami Palms Resort and Spa for their honeymoon. The reviews were stellar.

Mr. Gunther continued, "We're good at what we do because our entire staff operates as one. We're not a bunch of people moving in our own directions with our own goals. We move in the same direction toward one goal—creating a surreal customer experience. If we chose to go in different directions, it would be a total disaster. You certainly would not have chosen us."

He was probably right.

"So, Chris, what you need to do is operate as one, not two. It's how God designed marriage to work. Oneness is essential to move forward in your marriage and your money. It's the starting point for experience, contentment, and purpose."

"Okay. I think I understand," Chris said hesitantly.

Mr. Gunther reached back into his pockets and pulled out two tickets. "I want you and Claire to meet a very special, very rich couple that happens to be staying at the resort this week. These are complimentary tickets for our resort's suite at the sports arena. There's a basketball game tonight and they will be there."

Chris took the tickets. He was pumped. What a great opportunity, to enjoy a game and mingle with the rich. He couldn't wait to get back to the room to tell Claire.

"Thanks, Mr. Gunther!" Chris shook his hand.

Mr. Gunther smiled. "Of course. I'm glad you're here." Then in a more serious tone he said, "Chris, you have to decide to be one."

An Unfortunate Memory

I remember the moment clearly.

I was their banker. The middle-aged married couple sat in the two chairs on the other side of my office desk. I took one more glance at my computer screen, looked at their credit report, and then gave them the unfortunate news—their home loan application was denied. They had too many debts and not enough income. Their credit was maxed.

So they could understand what I was seeing, I began to read out loud the different debts listed on their credit report. As I read them, one by one, they acknowledged the debt with a reluctant head nod.

Until I read a particular credit card.

"That's not ours. Is it fraud?" questioned the wife.

"Possibly," I replied. As I began to walk them through the steps they should take to determine whether or not they were victims of identify theft, I saw something that the wife could not immediately see. Her husband's face had become very red, and beads of sweat were forming on his forehead.

"Just don't worry about it!" the husband suddenly exclaimed.

Understandably surprised, the wife quickly turned to the husband and said, "Why not? It's not ours."

"Just don't worry about it!" he repeated emphatically.

At this point, the wife saw what I had seen. Something was wrong. He was hiding something. While she did not recognize the card, he clearly did. What he had hoped would remain hidden in darkness had been brought to light.

The wife turned back to look at me, shocked, frustrated, sad, but calm. "I'm sorry, Art. We need to leave." And with that, she stood up and walked out of my office. Without saying a word, the husband followed behind her, his head lowered in shame.

I wish I knew what happened to that couple, but I don't. All I know is that a wedge had been driven down the middle of their relationship. The husband was on one side; the wife was on the other.

Years ago, when they said "I do," this was not a part of the marital plan. This was not part of the happily-ever-after dream.

It never is for any of us. And I know it isn't for you. You want something better. You want something more.

The Great Divider

Financial stress is taking its toll on us.

If at some point last month you found yourself stressed about money, you are not alone. In a survey on stress, the American Psychological Association found that money was the second (62%) highest source of stress among American adults. Thirty-four percent of respondents said they worry about unanticipated expenditures. Thirty percent worry about saving for retirement. And 25 percent worry about paying for essentials.[1]

Of course, financial stress does not stay contained to the individual. The stress seeps out and impacts our most important relationships, including our marriage.

I wish the statistics on money and divorce weren't so consistent, but they are. So I can't ignore them. And neither should you.

According to another study, 70 percent of couples admitted to arguing about money. These arguments are more frequent among younger couples than older couples. Why should we be concerned about money arguments? Because 57 percent of divorced couples reported that arguing over money was the reason for their divorce.[2] In fact, research reveals that fights about money are one of the leading predictors of future divorce.

With the consistent and abundant reporting on financial stress and its damaging effects on marriage, one would think that married couples would seek financial unity from day one of their marriage.

Unfortunately, statistics continue to reveal a different story.

Financial infidelity—lying about financial matters—isn't rare. In a Harris Poll, 42 percent of people said that they had committed financial infidelity. Seventy-five percent said that financial deception hurt their relationship.[3] Twenty-percent of respondents in a study from SunTrust said that they had spent $500 or more without their spouse knowing. Six percent confessed to hiding accounts from their spouse.[4]

While divorced couples may point to their finances as the reason for their divorce, there is normally more going on than meets the eye. Financial conflicts in marriage are usually symptoms of something more significant, something more foundational.

You may think there is no way that you will ever be one of these statistics, that you and your spouse are immune to this. I hope you are correct. But just remember this—very few couples get married thinking they will be a statistic one day.

I can guarantee that the couple in my bank office never thought they would be leaving a bank office, humiliated and hurt, because of financial infidelity.

This is the reality we are facing—marriages are being torn apart. And many couples are seeing the underlying issues manifest themselves in their finances.

This is not God's design for marriage. This is not God's design for money. You, your marriage, and your money were meant for more. You, your marriage, and your money were meant for something far greater, far more satisfying, far more adventurous, and far more lasting than you could ever imagine.

One

I have heard marriage compared to a pair of scissors. Two blades are united in a way that is never intended to separate. There are times when the blades may go in separate directions, pulling away from one another. But this movement does not allow for the scissors to operate as intended. Only when the two blades are brought together in unison do you experience the full potential of the scissors' design.

This is God's design for marriage—that two would become one. And their sacrificial love for one another would reflect God's sacrificial love. Marriage is a sacred union that, when following God's design, screams the gospel to the rest of the world.

It started in Genesis.

In Genesis 2:24, we see God setting the expectation that when a man and a woman enter into a marital relationship, two formerly separate entities are now united as one.

Paul writes about the depth of this oneness in 1 Corinthians 7:4: "A wife does not have the right over her own body, but her husband does. In the same way, a husband does not have the right over his own body, but his wife does."

In marriage, our rights over our own bodies are lost. Think about that statement for a moment. God's design for oneness in marriage runs so deep that our rights to our own bodies are null and void. In an act of incredible vulnerability, we relinquish our own authority and give ourselves to another.

Independence and individualism are valued in America. We value our autonomy and freedom. We want to do what we want, when we want to do it, and however we want to do it. And it is hard for these American values not to invade and warp our view of marriage.

But independence, individualism, autonomy, and personal freedom are not in God's design for marriage. The American value of independence must be laid aside, and sacrifice must be picked up in its place.

A rich marriage will not be found pursuing our own wants and desires. That path will only lead to greater discontent and division. A fulfilling in marriage will be found when two set aside their individual wants and desires for the sake of the one sacred union, in order for the world to know the one sacred God.

It is no longer "mine."

It is no longer "yours."

It is "ours."

And this oneness should seep into our marriage's finances.

More Than Money

God has an exciting design for our money, but most people are completely missing out on it.

You might be familiar with the parable of the talents in Matthew 25. The master was going on a journey and entrusted three servants with his possessions. The first servant received five talents, the second received two talents, and the third received one talent.

When the master returned, the servants reported how they managed his possessions. The first and second servant doubled what the master had given them, and they were rewarded accordingly. The third servant simply returned what he had been given, without any gain. The master sent him away because he had squandered the opportunity given to him.

We can learn four quick lessons from this parable:

1. **God owns everything.** The talents in the parable are always identified as the master's talents. No matter who is holding the possession, the ownership never changes.
2. **We are the managers.** God hands over some of his possessions for us to manage—or steward—well.
3. **Not everyone gets the same amount of possessions (and that's okay).** Some will be given more and some less. And

this is okay. Because it is not about the amount. It's about the stewardship.

4. **We are held accountable for whatever was entrusted to us.** Whether we have been given more or less, we will be held accountable for what we have been given.

But there is more here, something that is frequently missed.

This parable provides us with direction for the possessions under our watch. It is not merely stewardship for the sake of stewardship. When the master returned, the two celebrated servants had accomplished something very specific—they increased the master's wealth. The master returned to greater ownership than when he left. His kingdom had grown. His kingdom had advanced.

What does this tell us? Being a good manager of God's possessions doesn't mean just keeping them safe. That's boring. And keeping his possessions safe was exactly what the third servant did. We are called to something significantly more compelling.

Good stewardship that does not advance God's kingdom is not really good stewardship. There is a goal. There is a mission. There is a kingdom to advance. We are to be a part of advancing his kingdom. And this is exactly what God wants us to do with the possessions he has given us.

Good stewardship requires generosity.

God's Design for Money

Most of us chase things with our money that result in momentary satisfaction. We think if we can just buy that house, drive that car, wear those clothes, or even obtain financial independence, we will be satisfied and content.

But the satisfaction and content are short-lived. We buy that house with that car in the garage and those clothes in the closet. However, as the weeks, months, and years roll by, the luster is lost, and we are no longer satisfied with those things. We turn our attention to the next thing to satisfy.

I bet I can tell you of a time when you used money in a way that brought a greater, longer-lasting satisfaction.

It was when you used money for something greater than yourself.

You gave to your local church and its mission. You bought Christmas presents for a family you didn't know. You bought a backpack and school supplies for a child you would never meet. You helped a friend who got slammed with an unforeseen emergency.

I bet when you think back on that moment, you are hit with a sense of contentment and satisfaction. While you frequently regret past purchases, you rarely regret past generosity.

Why is that?

It is because when you are generous, you are getting closer to God's design for you and your money. You see, God designed us not to be hoarders but conduits through which his generosity flows.

Getting rid of debt is a good idea. Setting aside money for retirement is a good idea. Pursuing financial health is a good idea. And we will discuss those things in this book. But they are not for the ends in themselves. Being debt-free, having enough for retirement, and obtaining financial health are just means to a much greater, more exciting end.

They are a way for us to live the generous life he desires us to live. They are means to get us to a place where we can live with open hands, ready to give and go as God lead us. Financially healthy people are better able to say "yes" instead of "not yet."

This is why we pursue financial health.

The Dangerous Collision

So here we are—God has provided us a design for how our marriage and our money are to work. Yet, it is the collision of marriage and money that sends many couples reeling.

But it doesn't have to be this way.

What if, instead of seeing money as the great marriage divider, we saw it as the great marriage uniter? And what if the best way to make money a point of unity was to chase something bigger than either one of you? What if your motivation for financial health shifted away from the norm? What if you decided to leverage money not to just impact your marriage but to impact others as well? What if you decided to get financially healthy so that you could live with open hands, ready and willing to advance God's kingdom?

The collision of marriage and money doesn't have to result in arguments and divorce. The collision of marriage and money can enhance your understanding of why God put you two together in the first place. It can enhance your ability to make a difference in this world today and for all eternity. It may actually make you a strong, united force for the mission of advancing God's kingdom.

This book can help you take advantage of this collision that often hurts marriages and leverage it for the good of your marriage and your mission in life. We will discuss how you can obtain financial health, but not just for the sake of financial health. We will talk about obtaining financial health so that you and your spouse can experience the satisfying, openhanded, adventurous life that he designed you to live.

At the end of each chapter, you find Marriage Challenges. They are designed to get you both on the same financial page and to encourage you to live out God's design for you and your money. Many of them are simply conversation starters for you and your spouse.

I want you to be a rich couple. But this richness is not measured by dollars and cents. I want you to be rich in contentment and purpose. I want you and your marriage to be a part of something bigger than yourselves.

And I know that you want this. You want contentment and purpose in your marriage and finances.

Congratulations on your marriage—whether you're newly married, or you've been at this for decades. Welcome to The Marriage Challenge.

Let's get started.

Your Marriage Challenges

Day 1 Marriage Challenge: *Pray with your spouse.* Getting on the same financial page isn't always easy. You need God's help. Pray the following prayer together:

> *Help us be one. Help us experience the contentment and purpose you desire us to experience. Thank you for allowing us to be a part of your mission. Help us to steward your possessions well, leveraging them in order to advance your kingdom.*

Day 2 Marriage Challenge: *Have a conversation about money.* Use these marriage and money conversation starters:

1. Do you know someone who divorced over money issues? What was their story?

2. What are some of your money concerns?

3. What eternal difference do you want to make?

CHAPTER 2

Welcome to the Team

Chris and Claire entered the resort's suite at the arena. They had never felt more important at a game. Every time they showed their tickets to an arena staff member, the red carpet was rolled out.

"This is what it's like to be rich," whispered Chris to Claire as they opened the suite's door.

As they walked into the suite, a couple turned around and smiled. Chris and Claire smiled back. The couple did not fit the profile of people with great wealth. Their clothes were nothing spectacular; the wife's jewelry was surprisingly subtle and inexpensive. Fashion didn't seem to be important to them. They looked, well, ordinary.

"Chris and Claire! Welcome. It is so good to meet you. Come on in," exclaimed the husband. "My name is Terry, and this is my wife, Mary."

Terry shook Chris's hand and then Claire's hand. Mary did the same. They seemed to be genuinely excited to see them, and they were so full of life.

Mary waved Chris and Claire over. "Let's go over to our seats; they are about to do the national anthem and player introductions. Then we can get to know each other during the first quarter. The real action doesn't happen until later in the game anyway."

Terry laughed, "It's funny. My wife cares more about professional basketball than I do. She grew up a Chicago fan but has developed a love for Miami as well because we've attended so many games down here."

"It's true!" Mary said while patting Terry on the back.

As soon as the final player was introduced, Terry turned to Chris and Claire. "So tell me about you two."

Claire started, "Well, we're both from Charlotte, North Carolina. We met at a church there—Christ Community Church—and two years later our pastor married us. So now we're on our honeymoon."

"Congratulations!" said Terry.

"Thank you," Chris and Claire replied almost simultaneously, both with a half smile. Neither of their responses screamed enthusiasm, and both knew why.

Terry jumped back in, "Charlotte is a great place. Mary and I are from Chicago. She grew up there, and I moved to Chicago shortly after high school. We own an automotive repair shop in the area."

"We came up with a really original name—Terry's Auto Shop," Mary said jokingly.

Terry smiled, winked at Mary, and spoke, "You know, marriage can be tough. We certainly had our fair share of bumps. What I've learned is that marriage—not unlike basketball—is a team sport."

Chris and Claire looked at each other, not really knowing whether they were supposed to respond or not. Fortunately, Terry kept going.

Looking out onto the basketball court, he said, "Each of those players has to know and trust their teammates. They have to know their teammates' strengths and weaknesses so they can complement them. They have to know that their teammates have their back. And that they have their teammates' backs. Without knowledge of and trust in each other, the team would never win a game."

"Oneness," said Chris.

Claire looked at Chris inquisitively. She had not heard this word come out of Chris's mouth before.

"Mr. Gunther, the greeter who gave us the tickets, told me the importance of being one earlier," explained Chris.

"Exactly. Mr. Gunther is a wise man," said Terry.

"He also said you were a special, rich couple." As soon as Chris said this, he realized that the comment might not have been appropriate. This was common for Chris. He had been known to speak before thinking.

But before he could apologize, Mary spoke with a smile on her face, "That Mr. Gunther is also a funny man. I love him." She shook her head, the smile remaining on her face. "Look, we've learned the hard way. Both with our marriage and our money. It's only by God's grace that we had a few people in our path who pointed us to God's design for marriage and money."

Terry added, "Mary is my teammate. She's the one to whom I'm most loyal. I have her back, and I know that she has mine."

Chris liked the sound of that. So did Claire.

The group of four weren't paying attention to the game, so when the arena's buzzer sounded, they all jumped. The couples all laughed at how it startled them.

Terry spoke, "Hey, we usually have dinner on the balcony, outside of our room. There is plenty of space. We would love to have you over tonight."

"Sure. What room?" asked Chris.

Terry answered, "There's not really a room number. It's just the seventh floor. They made the entire floor one suite. Trust me, we have more than enough room for dinner guests. Don't worry. I'm not cooking. The food is from the resort."

"That sounds great," interjected Claire with a smile.

Marriage, Money, and Rowing

Like many kids, I grew up playing sports. Though I was not a star athlete, never receiving any college recruiting letters, I had fun playing baseball, basketball, and football, while dabbling in cross-country and volleyball.

Not surprisingly, my kids are now playing sports—baseball, basketball, and soccer. Do I think they will grow up to be professional athletes? I'm not counting on it. But I still encourage them to play, to get out on the field or court and give it their all.

Why?

Certainly, there are health benefits for them. And it does help my sanity, getting them out of the house. But the biggest driver of my encouragement is the life lessons that are often taught through sports—one of which is what it means to be on a team.

When you are on an athletic team, you learn how to work with people from different backgrounds, with different mind-sets, strengths, and weaknesses. You learn how to complement those on your team, when to step up and when to step back. You learn to celebrate together, and you learn to face disappointment together.

When it's game time, you have your teammates' backs, and they have yours. You are confident in it. You rely on it.

Until the game clock hits zero, you operate as one. Or at least the most successful teams do.

While I played several sports growing up, I never rowed; rowing was never an option at our school. But recently, I have become fascinated with the sport—not actually participating but learning about and from it.

The number of individuals in a particular boat can vary, but the nine-person crews capture most of my attention. In these boats, eight of the nine individuals sit with their back turned away from the race's finish line. These are the ones with the oars. They are the boat's engine. The ninth individual is the only one who faces the finish line. He or she can see what every other crew member cannot see. He or she is the one with the rudder, the one who can guide the boat. He or she is the one who tells the other eight to maintain or speed up.

The eight must be in complete sync with one another. Their oars must hit the water at the exact same time and at the exact same angle. A simple, unintentional flick of the wrist can throw off the entire boat's momentum. Because of this, a crew member who attempts to stand out and somehow set himself or herself apart from the rest of the crew will devastate the crew's chance of succeeding. Rowing requires total personal sacrifice, and because of this, some call it the ultimate team sport.

Success requires placing the team above the self.

In marriage, your spouse is your teammate. You are in the boat together. You celebrate together. You face disappointment together. And the marriage will operate best when you find yourself in sync with your teammate.

Like rowing, there is only one who can see the end. And you must trust the One who sees the finish line and everything else.

It is not you.

It is not your teammate.

It is God.

He knows what needs to be done in order to achieve success, to win this race.

This is one of the most important teams you will ever be a part of, and how you play the game will impact far more than one season. Sometimes, you will have to sacrifice for the betterment of the team. Because it should always be team above self.

Couples who experience contentment and purpose in their marriage are great teammates. They are rich because they are one.

Your Team Number One

Patrick Lencioni is an author best known for his business fables. It is from his writings that I first learned about a concept he dubbed "Team Number One."

In the business context, here is how you identify your Team Number One—they are those included in your highest-level meeting. So if you are included in an executive meeting, with the president and vice presidents, this group is probably your Team Number One.

Why is it important to identify your Team Number One?

Your Team Number One receives your loyalty. Certainly, there will be times of disagreement. In fact, unanimity on most decisions will be rare. But the disagreements and debates stay in the meeting. They stay within the team. You state your opinion, debate, and then decide. Of course, this means that some give-and-take must occur in the meeting. But here is the key—when you leave the meeting, you stand united with your Team Number One.

You have their back, and they have your back. You are each other's priority relationship.

In marriage, you and your teammate (your spouse) are your Team Number One. You have their back and they have your back. Outside of your relationship with God, your teammate in marriage is your priority relationship.

This means there will be times of disagreement. There will be times of debate. But when the dust settles, you stand together. You are united. You protect that unity. You sacrifice for that unity. God designed marriage for that type of unity.

Not Your Team Number One

I love my kids. If you were to ask me what I would do for them, my immediate response would be, "Anything."

I love my parents. I am incredibly grateful to have been raised by two God-fearing parents. They mean the world to me.

And you probably feel the same way. Well, not about *my* kids and parents but *your* kids (or future kids) and parents.

However, neither of these categories of people are my Team Number One.

With the best of intentions, couples sometimes find themselves shifting their loyalty away from their teammate and toward their children or parents. For example, you agree on a spending limit for your son's birthday presents. But then he isolates one of his parents and begs, pleads, even cries because he wants a toy so badly for his birthday. The problem is that the toy exceeds the dollar amount you and your teammate set. Instead of consulting with your other Team Number One member, you fold to the feelings of guilt and pity. You agree to get the more expensive present.

Your loyalty shifted.

Or consider your parents. You and your spouse decide to buy a used SUV that fits your budget. When you mention this in a conversation with your parents, instead of approval they express disappointment. They don't understand why you would buy a used car. They never bought used cars. They feel that you are being too conservative with your money and encourage you to get a new, more expensive car. They sound pretty convincing, and so you team up with your parents and try to convince your spouse that a new car is the better decision.

Your loyalty shifted.

You may have already experienced the results of these shifts in loyalty. You may have been the one who shifted loyalty, and the result was a frustrated and disappointed teammate. Or you may be the one from whom the loyalty shifted, and the result was a sense of hurt and betrayal.

When it comes to marriage and money, loyalty to your Team Number One is vital. A lack of loyalty will quickly cause a meltdown not just of financial health but of marital health.

Kids are great. Parents are great. Love both groups well. But make sure that they do not infiltrate your Team Number One. Make sure your loyalty, your primary commitment, lies with your spouse.

As you progress in your finances, as you dream together and plan together, expect disagreement and healthy debate. But when you are done, be committed to a unified front which friends, kids, or parents cannot overcome.

Be committed. Be loyal. Be one.

Put It on the Table

Surprises can be fun. My wife once threw a surprise birthday party for me, and I loved it.

But some surprises are not fun. Finding out that your teammate has a significant amount of debt is one of those types of surprises. These are surprises to avoid.

You may have bank accounts, credit cards, student loans, car debts, and even a mortgage. Your teammate has their accounts, cards, and loans. One of the first steps to deciding to be one—if you have not done so already—is to put it all on the table.

Gather all of your financial information—even your credit score. Ask your teammate to do the same. Then sit down and go through everything, ugly debts and all.

Seeing the totality of your financial situation is key to progressing in your financial health. The conversation is not always enjoyable, but it is absolutely necessary. You would not attempt to climb a mountain without first studying its terrain. Knowing the terrain helps you chart the best path. Similarly, you need to know what you are up against as a couple so that you can chart the best path.

Put everything on the table so you can make the best decisions together moving forward.

Get Your Accounts Together

One of the best initial steps for a couple pursuing financial unity is to join your accounts. If a joint account is not an option (e.g., retirement accounts), make sure your spouse has the ability to access it. Sometimes this may be as simple as providing a user identification and password.

While dating, you had separate accounts. More than likely, neither had access to the other's account. And this made sense. You were two separate units.

But then you said, "I do." And two became one. You didn't say "I do" to only part of your spouse, and your spouse didn't say "I do" to only part of you. It was an all-in deal.

And that includes your finances.

Making sure that both spouses have access to every financial account is not just a good practical way to get on the same page. Joint accounts communicate something to your spouse—that they are your Team Number One.

Joint accounts communicate that your money is now "our money." The statement "Well, it's my money so . . ." creates a sense of division. When you put your accounts together, it sends a message that you really are one, including your finances. It does not matter who makes more or less money for the family. It is both the husband's and the wife's money—every single penny.

Joint accounts communicate unity. Every purchase makes up "our expenditures." Your purchases affect your spouse. If you have poor purchase habits, your spouse will feel the financial burden that results from them. Married couples do not make financial decisions in a vacuum. Joint accounts encourage involvement from both husband and wife when determining purchases.

Joint accounts communicate transparency. When you have joint accounts, there's no hiding. It tells your spouse you want them to be aware of your purchases. You are communicating that no expenditure or movement of money is done in secret.

Joint accounts communicate trust. You have confidence in them, and they have confidence in you. You believe that both will make money decisions in an agreed-upon way.

Joint accounts communicate commitment. Contrastingly, separate accounts communicate that there are parts of you that are off-limits. These accounts may demonstrate a desire to remain free from accountability to one another. Combining your money shows a raised level of commitment. You are committed to your spouse. You are one. Every part of you is theirs, including every penny in the bank account.

Marriage is an all-in deal. This is how God designed your marriage to operate. Bring your accounts together. Make your finances reflect oneness.

Welcome to the Team

So, welcome to the team. You have your strengths, and your spouse has their strengths. You have your weaknesses, and they have their weaknesses. You have your preferences, and they have their preferences. This should not create concern but excitement as you lean on one another toward your financial goals.

There will be moments of struggle. There will be moments of sacrifice. And if done well, there will be moments of celebration.

You were meant for more. Your marriage was meant for more. And your money was meant for more.

Be loyal to your Team Number One. And, as a team, trust in God's guidance for your marriage and your money.

———————

Your Marriage Challenges

Day 3 Marriage Challenge: *Put everything on the table.* Gather all of your financial accounts. Spend some time going through them with your spouse. Make sure both of you know about every account.

Day 4 Marriage Challenge: *Have a team huddle.* Use these marriage and money conversation starters:

1. What has been your favorite team of which you have been a part and why? (And no, you can't say your spouse.)

2. Why does the Team Number One concept matter to you?

3. What will it take to make sure you both have access to all financial accounts?

CHAPTER 3

Your Money Story

Chris and Claire went back to their room to clean up before dinner. Attending the game helped get their mind off their earlier argument. For a moment, it was as if it never happened. For a moment, everything seemed right.

For a moment.

But then Chris looked at the chair in which he was sitting when Claire first told him about the debt. The earlier fight flooded his mind. And all the anger made its return.

"You should have told me earlier," Chris said with a frustrated tone. He sat down on the edge of the bed.

Claire was in the bathroom, trying to comb the Miami humidity out of her hair.

"What do you want me to do, Chris? I told you I'm sorry, that I should have told you about it before. I can't go back and fix it now. What, would you have changed your mind about marrying me if you knew about the debt?" She angrily yanked the comb through her hair.

Chris didn't respond, which didn't sit well with Claire.

"You're a jerk!" yelled Claire.

Still sitting on the edge of the bed, Chris was now slouched over, his head in his hands. Suddenly, a memory rushed into mind. Three Christmases ago, his brother had a huge blowup with his wife, right in front of the family. The argument was over how much they had spent on Christmas gifts. His brother thought it was too much. She thought he was unnecessarily cheap and didn't care about others. He remembered her words before she left the house, slamming the door behind her.

"You're a jerk!"

Having Claire use the same words bothered him deeply.

Chris did not want his marriage to end like his brother's. He remembered thinking during the Christmas argument that they were probably both a little right and a little wrong. More than likely, reality was somewhere in between. They just needed to hear each other out. Chris knew why his brother was cheap, and he empathized. His wife probably had her reasons for wanting to get everyone a nice gift. If only they had listened to one another.

Calmly, Chris spoke. "Claire, do you know why I hate debt?"

"Because you listen to Dave Ramsey."

That gave him a slight smile. "Yes, but there's more. I grew up with parents who lived paycheck to paycheck because they had a ton of debt. Even until this day, I have never seen my parents without a crippling load of debt hanging over them. My brother and I hated it. We used to talk about it growing up. We would not be like them."

Chris took a quick pause before he continued, "I feel like my parents are missing out on something because of their finances. And I just want more. I want to break the cycle."

He remembered Mr. Gunther's words. "I want contentment and purpose."

There was silence in the room for a few minutes. Both were trying to get their emotions under control.

Then, Claire walked out of the bathroom and gently responded, "Chris, I want that too. I want it in our marriage and in our finances. Look, I didn't tell you about the debt because I was scared. I'm scared of the debt, and I was scared how you would respond. I just didn't know what to do. I should have told you. I wish I would have known that about your family. I guess we all have our own money stories."

"I guess we do."

Claire sat next to Chris on the bed's edge. Chris's head remained in his hands. His eyes stared at the floor.

"I want to be a good teammate for you, for our finances, and for our marriage," said Chris. "I want this marriage to work. I want our team to work."

Claire looked at Chris, "Let's finish getting ready. Terry and Mary are waiting on us."

The Experience Effect

In late 1929, the stock market began to tumble downward. The tumble created a panic, and the market crashed. Banks closed their doors, companies went out of business, and people lost their jobs.

This began the era from 1929 to 1939 known as the Great Depression. During this time fifteen million people were unemployed, around a 25 percent unemployment rate. Many lived with hunger and most lived with fear.

You may have known someone who lived during the Great Depression—maybe your grandparents or great-grandparents. And if you were to tell me about the way they managed their money, you would probably mention that they were very frugal people.

Such a comment is common when describing those who lived through the Great Depression. Their past experiences influenced their present mind-set.

Generations are not only known for being born during a certain time period. Generations are also known for their shared characteristics. Of course, this does not mean that everyone who is a part of the

Millennial generation will be exactly the same. But there will be some commonalities found.

How does this happen?

Part of the answer is shared experiences. Shared experiences often result in shared characteristics.

Consider the Millennial generation. They are the generation who grew up seeing reports of school shootings, watching the Twin Towers fall, and witnessing either their parents or themselves lose money and jobs as the market plummeted in 2008.

Experiences like these had an impact on Millennials' thinking. From a money standpoint, Millennials tend to be less eager to invest in the stock market; only one in three do so.[1] They also tend to have less confidence in their employers, so they act and work more independently, relying on themselves to make career advancement decisions and earn greater income.

Those who lived through the Great Depression tended to be passionate about saving and distrustful of financial institutions. They would often hide money in their houses, under their mattresses, or buried in their backyard. They did a great job of living within their means and avoiding debt.

Each generation is shaped by their shared experiences.

And while this is true on the generational level, personal experiences influence us on the individual level as well. You and your spouse's past money experiences influence the way you think about money today.

What Is Your Story?

My wife and I grew up with different money experiences. Neither was right or wrong, just different.

I have early childhood memories of getting food from our church's food pantry because we did not have money to purchase food. My wife had no such childhood memory. I grew up in a house where I was encouraged to start preparing for retirement and open a Roth IRA when I was around sixteen or seventeen years old. My wife's experience was different.

Both of us grew up in homes that modeled and encouraged generosity—sometimes extravagant generosity. Our experiences shaped our understanding and view of money.

So, what is your story?

Think back on your past. What were your experiences with money? There were probably some significant, national, money-related events that you experienced. If you are Millennials, your experiences may include the 2008 market downturn.

But what about on a more personal level?

Did you witness your parents struggle to pay the bills?

Did you see your parents get crushed by a load of debt?

Or was money just not an issue and spending frequent?

What about the conversations you had growing up? Did they include advice on giving generously, saving wisely, and living appropriately? Or did no such conversation occur?

These experiences undoubtedly shaped your way of thinking. And they shaped your spouse's way of thinking as well.

Of course, similar experiences may affect different people in different ways. The experience of having little may influence someone to better understand the value of a dollar. On the other hand, a similar experience may influence someone to prioritize money and materialism.

Combine the influence of these experiences with you and your spouse's natural personality, and you begin to get close to understanding you and your teammate's money personalities.

Why is it important to understand your money personalities?

Empathy. When you are empathetic toward your teammate's money personality, you can better understand where he or she is coming from when making money decisions.

The Four Money Personalities

We all have a money personality. And each money personality has its strengths and weaknesses. More than likely, yours will differ from your spouse's. God seems to regularly team us up like this.

Consider the following four money personalities:

The Spender

Spenders find pleasure in swiping the debit or credit card. They pay first and worry about consequences later. Motivations for spending may vary. Some spend because it simply gives them a rush. Purchasing something makes them feel good. Some spend because they like to give gifts. They enjoy watching the recipient of their gift light up when they tear apart the wrapping paper. Others spend to boost their ego. When they are out with friends, they are the ones who pay for everyone to demonstrate how successful they are.

Spender strengths. Spenders are often referred to in a negative manner. But there are real strengths to be found in spenders. First of all, they are actually willing to pull the trigger when a purchase needs to be made. Second, they are the ones who are often thinking about and planning gift purchases for birthdays, anniversaries, and Christmas. Because of this, they are often good at maintaining relationships.

Spender weaknesses. Spending can get the best of them and their budget. Spenders can quickly erode what money is left in a bank account. They can also be prone to credit card debt. The overarching weakness of spenders is the lack of value they place on money. Money is something they are quick to dispose of.

The Saver

Savers get excited when they see the amount in their savings or retirement account go up. They are uncertain about the future, so they want to prepare well for whatever it may bring. Savers also tend to be passionate about paying down debt. Like saving money, reducing debt helps give savers a greater sense of financial security.

Saver Strengths. The saver personality tends to be the most celebrated money personality. This admiration occurs because savers often make good financial decisions—saving for emergencies and paying off debt. Savers are often viewed as having the safest of the money personalities.

Saver Weaknesses. Like any money personality, savers can go to an unhealthy extreme. Savers can become frugal beyond what is necessary. They can suck the life out of life. They opt for a tent instead of a hotel room on the family vacation, not because they can't afford a hotel room but simply because it costs money. Savers are also more prone to give a guilt trip when money is spent—"A roof over little Billy's head is enough of a birthday present for him." And some savers are hesitant to put money into the stock market, even for retirement purposes, because they fear losing money.

The Investor

Investors are willing to take risks with money. This is not always a bad thing. For example, they have no problem putting money in the stock market. They are willing to ride out the downturns in the market for long-term gains. They can also be entrepreneurial, attempting to start their own business. They believe that in order to make money, you have to spend money. They are always searching for a good return on their money.

Strengths. Investors invest. They are willing to do what is necessary (investing) to have enough for retirement and other future needs. They understand how money can be leveraged to accomplish greater things. They are usually pretty optimistic and are confident about their ability to make money.

Weaknesses. Investors can get carried away with the allure of higher returns. Their confidence can turn into overconfidence. When this happens, they get financially reckless. The potential of a great return can sometimes cause them to disregard sound financial practices.

The Ignorer

You've seen images of ostriches with their head in the ground. When it comes to money, ignorers react in a similar manner. They get really uncomfortable. They don't want to talk about money, listen to anything about money, or deal with anything that has to do with money. Ignorers constantly try to postpone money issues, hoping they will eventually go away.

Strengths. Ignorers are willing to trust others, whether it is their spouse or a financial professional, to manage their money. When married, they rarely get into heated conversations about money. They are often willing to sacrifice their preference for the preference of their spouse.

Weaknesses. Ignorers are unaware of their financial standing. Do they have too much debt? Are they saving enough? They simply don't know. Such a position is very dangerous. Never expressing their preference can build up resentment and anger. Avoiding the smaller, heated disagreements can eventually lead to one big nuclear argument.

Which One Are You?

So, what is your money personality? You may not fit perfectly into one specific category, but you at least have leanings toward one or two of them. Understanding your and your spouse's money personality will be extremely beneficial when having conversations about money.

My wife leans more toward the Saver money personality. Ensuring that we have enough money set aside for an emergency is important to her, and she doesn't like financial risks. Because I know this about her, I am not surprised when she mentions that she would like to increase our savings. In fact, I expect it. Since we are a team, I allow her money personality and financial priorities to influence my priorities, both in decision making and conversations.

This is what good teammates do.

Knowing your and your spouse's money personality can help you do the same thing.

A fun way to get a sense of your money personality is to imagine that you just received a financial windfall. Let's say a grocery store identifies you as the one-millionth customer. Balloons drop. Confetti rains. The grocery store's staff cheers. You feel awkward, but out walks the store manager with a $50,000 check. Congratulations, you just won $50,000.

What will you do with it?

Will it go to retirement? How about paying off your student loan debt? Or what about a portion of your mortgage? What about a vacation? Would you want to purchase some extravagant gifts for your friends?

The way you answer this question should tell you something about your money personality.

Fill Gaps

The great philosopher Sylvester Stallone graced us with this quote in the movie *Rocky*—"She's got gaps. I've got gaps. Together, we fill gaps."

Your money background and your money personality have strengths and weaknesses. You teammate's money background and money personality have strengths and weaknesses. You have gaps. Your teammate has gaps. And now you need to figure out how to work together to fill gaps.

Here are a few questions for you to get started:

What is my teammate's money background and money personality? It starts here. Understanding their past and personality is critical to understanding who they are in the present.

How does this differ from my money background and money personality? Compare and contrast. Most couples can identify both similarities and differences.

To be a good teammate, what sacrifices might I have to make? Don't start with where you would like your spouse to sacrifice or fill gaps. Start with yourself. What might you have to sacrifice? What gaps can you fill? Good teammates put team above self.

What financial roles best fit our money personalities? There are different money tasks in your marriage. Someone needs to pay the bills. Someone needs to do the taxes. Someone needs to keep the budget. Who is best suited for the various money roles? The earlier you match the right roles with the right personality, the better off you will be.

Your story matters. So does your teammate's. Take some time to consider both, and get ready to move forward with God's design for you and your money.

Your Marriage Challenges

Day 5 Marriage Challenge: *Memorize Psalm 139:14 together.* Your money personality is not a mistake. God has shaped you in a unique way. You are fearfully and wonderfully made. And so is your spouse.

Day 6 Marriage Challenge: *Have a conversation about your money personalities.* Use these marriage and money conversation starters:

1. How do you view money? What one personal memory had a big impact on how you view money?

2. What is your money personality? What one personal story can you tell that demonstrates this?

3. What would you do if you won $50,000 today?

4. As it relates to your money personality, what gaps do you need help filling? What gaps can you help fill?

CHAPTER 4

Become a Millionaire

Chris and Claire had never seen a "room" like this. It was amazing in every way. The suite was huge, equipped with a pool table, baby grand piano, and a massive television. The furniture was so nice they felt like it was meant for viewing instead of using, like someone was going to jump out and scold them for touching it.

And they were not exaggerating about having enough room on the balcony. It spanned the entire floor. Before, when they looked up at the building, Chris and Claire assumed that the seventh floor balcony was for a number of rooms, not one suite. They were wrong.

Chris thought, *Wow. They really are the rich couple.*

"This place is amazing!" Chris exclaimed. "I've never seen anything like this in real life. I feel like I'm in a movie. You guys are actually evil villains, aren't you?"

Terry and Mary laughed.

"Quite the opposite, I hope," replied Terry, still smiling.

Just then, the suite's door opened. To Chris and Claire's surprise, it was Mr. Gunther.

"Am I okay to come in?"

"Of course, Mr. Gunther! Come on in. It's so good to see you," Mary said happily as she gave him a hug.

"Are you enjoying your stay? Is the room okay?" asked Mr. Gunther.

Mary said, "You know it is. Everything about this place is always perfect. Thank you."

Mr. Gunther turned to Chris and Claire. "And how you are you two?"

"We are pretty amazed at this place," Chris responded with a grin.

"I'm glad you like it. That really means a lot to me. Now your dinner will be here shortly. If I can do anything for any of you, let me know."

"We will. Again, thank you for everything," said Mary.

Right as Mr. Gunther left the suite, four staff members entered the room with their dinner. They quickly took the food out to the balcony and set it on the table. After they poured the drinks, they left. Chris continued to be impressed by the resort staff. They excelled at creating a great experience.

"Oneness," he whispered to himself.

They went outside and enjoyed the meal the resort staff brought. It was a perfect night. Eating on the massive balcony, savoring incredible food, listening to the ocean's waves as they played background music—it was a surreal experience for Chris and Claire.

As they finished dinner, they all walked to the edge of the balcony to look out onto the ocean.

"Wow. What an amazing journey God has allowed us to be a part of," said Terry with his hands placed on the balcony's railing. "What a satisfying adventure he has put us on."

"Yes. It seems like God has blessed you guys a lot," said Chris as he looked out over the beach.

"He has," replied Terry. "It's amazing what can happen when you stop trying to accumulate a bunch of stuff for yourself and, instead, start trying to use your resources to help others and make an eternal impact." Terry looked at Chris. "You know, one of the big turning points in our marriage and our finances was when we started chasing something much bigger than ourselves. We decided that we were going to get our finances in order, not to get a bigger house but to expand our capacity to live generously."

Chris was a little surprised by his comments.

Terry continued, "We found contentment and purpose in both our marriage and money by chasing God's design and being a part of his mission. Wealth is not unimportant. Financial health matters. But it isn't the most important thing by far. I know a lot of guys with a lot of money who are totally dissatisfied with life. At the same time I know guys who have little, yet are completely content. I've seen people point to money as the reason for their marriage problems. It's funny though, the purpose for my and Mary's money brings us together."

Chris replied, "Maybe it's not about the money."

Terry looked at Mary, who was still looking out at the beach. Terry smiled, nodded his head in agreement, and said one word, "Exactly."

Marriage and Wealth

Millionaire.

Admittedly, I was hesitant to include this chapter. God's ultimate goal for providing money is not for us to be wealthy but to use whatever wealth we do have to advance his kingdom. It is a contentment-filled, adventurous journey, and you don't want to miss out.

I don't want you to substitute the pursuit of wealth for the pursuit of God's design for your money. Wealth is not bad. But putting our hope in wealth makes it an idol. In 1 Timothy 6:17–19, Paul says:

> Instruct those who are rich in the present age not to be
> arrogant or to set their hope on the uncertainty of wealth,
> but on God, who richly provides us with all things to

enjoy. Instruct them to do what is good, to be rich in good
works, to be generous and willing to share, storing up treasure for themselves as a good foundation for the coming
age, so that they may take hold of what is truly life.

God can and will use wealth to accomplish his mission. And
these verses instruct those with much how to leverage their resources
for kingdom purposes—be generous, share, do good works, store up
treasures in heaven.

I want you to get a fresh perspective on what could be, not even
for your own sake, but for the sake of others who will be impacted by
your generosity.

Most assume that the term *millionaire* could never apply to them.
They defeat themselves before they even start.

But what if the term *millionaire* wasn't what you thought it was?
What if being a millionaire was more attainable that you realize? Not
easy. But attainable.

My hope is that this chapter motivates and inspires you to pursue
financial health and helps you understand what is possible when you
do.

I believe that many of you can be millionaires one day. And you
will be able to use your resources to live generously and advance God's
kingdom in ways you never imagined.

Sometimes it's just a matter of being ordinary.

How Much Are You Worth?

If your mom or dad responded to this question, their answer
would probably be "priceless." And there is probably not much you
could do to change that.

But when this question is presented in the context of money, the
answer will differ slightly. Okay, it will differ a lot. And usually the
question is worded like this—*What is your net worth?* Of course, before

you can answer that question, you must know what this term, *net worth*, actually means.

So, what is net worth?

I'm sure you are familiar with the word *worth*. You've probably asked the question "How much is that worth?" many times. When using *worth* in a financial conversation, it means the value of something in terms of dollars and cents. For example, that house is *worth* $200,000.

Net is a math word. It means remaining after, usually following some type of deduction. Like five minus four leaves us with a net of one.

So let's put these two words together.

Net worth is the difference between your assets (the value of what you own) and your liabilities (how much you owe). Your goal should be to own more than you owe, resulting in a positive net worth.

You can calculate your net worth by adding up the value of your bank accounts, retirement accounts, home, automobiles, and anything else of significant value. Then subtract any loans (including the mortgage) and credit card balances. The final number should give you a good idea of your net worth.

Why is it important to know your net worth? Your net worth gives you a good indication of your financial health.

Consider this example. Your friend says that their assets, the value of what they own, look like this:

- House: $300,000
- Automobiles: $25,000
- Bank accounts: $5,000
- Retirement: $10,000

Therefore, their assets total $340,000. Pretty good, right? Maybe. It's too early to tell.

Your friend then tells you their liabilities, what they owe.

- Mortgage: $290,000
- Car loans: $20,000
- Student loans: $20,000
- Credit cards: $12,000

So their total liabilities total $342,000. This means that their net worth (assets minus liabilities) is -$2,000. This is not good. While the lifestyle they portray may feign financial health, your friend is actually in a financial hole. They owe more than they own.

Why is your net worth so important?

First, your net worth is probably one of the most accurate indicators of your financial health. Many people create an image of being wealthy by purchasing expensive homes, cars, vacations, and clothes with debt. But this is just a façade that will eventually catch up with them. Net worth breaks through the appearance of wealth and reveals real wealth.

Second, net worth helps you maintain perspective. It really doesn't matter if you live in a $300,000 house if you owe $300,000 on it. It looks nice, but looking nice does not make you any wealthier and will not help you in the future. However, avoiding mortgages (and therefore houses) that stretch your finances, paying down debt, and setting aside money for emergencies and retirement can make you wealthier.

Finally, net worth is an easy way to gauge your progress. Getting a general idea of your net worth does not take much work. We just did it in the above example. You can easily check your net worth to monitor if your financial health is going in the right direction. If your net worth is going up, you are going in the right direction. It really is that simple.

To increase your net worth, you have two options—increase your assets or decrease you liabilities. For most it needs to be a combination of the two. Money should be set aside for the future, and debt needs to be eliminated. (You probably didn't realize that paying off a credit card would make you wealthier, did you?)

Both are important and both will make you wealthier.

What $1,000,000 Really Looks Like

When you think of a millionaire, what images come to mind? Is it a person driving around in a black Lamborghini, the one he only takes out of the garage a few times a year? Is it someone sitting on her house's deck in Beverly Hills, overlooking the city below? Or is it someone lying on the beach in Bora Bora, a place they regularly frequent?

These images make the idea of being a millionaire seem unattainable. You feel so far away from that lifestyle that you think you will never be within reach.

I am not going to try to convince you that you can one day drive a Lamborghini, own a house in Beverly Hills, and vacation in Bora Bora regularly. In fact, I am not convinced those types of expenditures best align you with God's design for you and your money. However, I do want to demonstrate that being a millionaire is not something reserved for those we just described. Being a real millionaire probably looks a lot different than you think.

So set aside those images for a minute. What is a real millionaire?

A millionaire is someone with a net worth of one million dollars. That's it. The definition of a millionaire does not relate to vacations taken, cars driven, or houses lived in. A millionaire just needs to have a net worth of $1,000,000.

Why is understanding this important? Because millionaire status is probably more attainable than you realize.

Let's say a young couple decided to give generously, save wisely, and live appropriately. They committed to avoiding debt (except for their mortgage) and living below their means so they could set aside money for retirement and pay off their mortgage.

When they first got married, their net worth looked something like this:

Assets ($271,000)
- House: $250,000
- Automobiles: $6,000
- Bank accounts: $5,000
- Retirement: $10,000

Liabilities ($220,000)
- Mortgage: $200,000
- Student loan debt: $20,000

Net Worth ($51,000)
- Assets – Liabilities

So they have a net worth of $51,000. Not a bad start. Over the next forty years of their marriage, they did not waiver on their plan. When they turned sixty-five years old and were considering retirement, their net worth looked something like this:

Assets ($1,405,000)
- House: $350,000
- Automobiles: $25,000
- Bank accounts: $30,000
- Retirement: $1,000,000

Liabilities ($0)

Net Worth ($1,405,000)
- Assets – Liabilities

Because they do not owe anything, their net worth at sixty-five years old is $1,405,000. They are millionaires.

Now, did they start out as millionaires? No. Did they become millionaires overnight? No, it was a long process. Did they live the lifestyle that most image millionaires live? Of course not. This couple simply made sure to pay off their all their debt and set aside money for retirement.

If you are a couple starting out, these numbers—specifically the retirement number—may seem daunting. They are not. You can do this too. And in the upcoming chapters, we will learn how.

Just Your Average Millionaire

The Millionaire Next Door was first published in 1996. I still remember the first time I read the book as it radically altered the way I perceived millionaires. Before I read that book, I viewed millionaires as Lamborghini-driving, Beverly Hills-living, Bora Bora-vacationing people. The book spends most of the time discussing the practices of those who have a net worth between $1 million and $10 million.

One of the immediate findings that jumped out to me was that most millionaires are first-generation millionaires. This means that they did not get their wealth from an inheritance; they built it up over time. This should encourage many, if not most, who do not come from a financially well-to-do background.

You would not be able to identify most millionaires from outward appearances and purchases. Those who actually have a net worth of a million or more are usually pretty frugal. They buy cheap suits and opt for a preowned, everyday automobile as opposed to a new, exotic car. The most commonly driven automobile by millionaires according to *The Millionaire Next Door* was a preowned Ford pickup truck. They don't buy items to show off their financial status to the world.

Real millionaires spend less than they make. This habit ensures wealth building. They do not view their salary as their spending limit. They cap their spending well below their salary. And this makes sense. The margin between your income and your expenses is where you build wealth. It is very difficult to increase your net worth if you are always spending every dollar that hits your bank account.

The book also revealed that those with a net worth between $1 million and $10 million understand the importance of wise investing. They understand that risk is necessary to get the return needed to have enough set aside for retirement. Keeping future retirement money in a savings account would not get them where they needed to be.

This is the picture of a real millionaire. Most of the time you would have no way to identify them as wealthy. They wear ordinary clothes, drive ordinary cars, and live in ordinary homes. Yet it is exactly because of their ordinary ways that they are millionaires.

Over time they increased their net worth by spending less than they earned, paying off debt, and setting aside money for the future.

You probably know the story of the tortoise and the hare. This Aesop's fable is where we get the phrase, "Slow and steady wins the race." The tortoise wins through persistence. He doesn't give up. He just keeps doing what he needs to do.

Average millionaires can relate better to the tortoise than the hare. Their story is one of remaining slow and steady. When the world around them was elevating status symbols as a way to demonstrate success, average millionaires just kept doing what they needed to do.

Act Like a Future Average Millionaire

You are closer to being a future millionaire than you realize, but the journey is not always easy or popular. In our society instant gratification—the desire to get what we want when we want it—is everywhere. But this will not help you get your net worth to $1 million. Acting like the popular images of millionaires when you don't have the money to do so almost ensures that you will never actually be a millionaire. You get there by starting early, paying off debt, and setting aside money for the future. And then, over time, you will be able to increase your net worth.

Is being a millionaire the ultimate goal for your life? Not at all. Should it even be the ultimate goal for your finances? No. Your ultimate financial goal is to bring God glory and advance his kingdom with your resources.

But being an average millionaire usually means you have a house without a mortgage, and you have enough for retirement—two achievements that, if stewarded well, can help you bring God glory and advance his kingdom with your resources. And since the combination of these two achievements usually gets you close to a $1 million net worth, I hope that everyone can one day be just an ordinary, boring, average millionaire.

Your Marriage Challenge

Day 7 Marriage Challenge: *Have a conversation about net worth.* Use these marriage and money conversation starters:

1. What do you think your net worth is?

2. What thoughts run through your mind when you learn about the average millionaire?

3. What would be the best way to increase your net worth?

Decide to Chase after God's Design for Your Money Together

Contentment and purpose. How can these things come about through our finances? They happen when couples decide to use their money for something bigger than themselves, to chase God-sized dreams. Get financially healthy but not for the sake of financial health. That's boring. Get financially healthy because it allows you to live more generously and advance his kingdom. And when you are living generously and advancing his kingdom, you will experience the purposeful and contentment-filled life God intended for you to experience.

Coming up, you have eight Money Milestones to guide you to a financially healthy, generous life.

They are:

Milestone 1: Start giving.

Milestone 2: Save $1,500 for a minor emergency.

Milestone 3: Max out your 401(k) or 403(b) match.

Milestone 4: Pay off all debt except your mortgage.

Milestone 5: Save three to six months of living expenses for a job-loss emergency.

Milestone 6: Put 15 percent of your gross income into retirement.

Milestone 7: Save for college or pay off your mortgage.

Milestone 8: Live generously.

Go after them together.

CHAPTER 5

It All Starts with Generosity

Claire decided to sleep in, so Chris was eating breakfast by himself.

"Good morning, Mr. Chris. How was dinner last night?" asked Mr. Gunther.

Chris was surprised to see Mr. Gunther at the resort's restaurant so early.

"Do they ever let you have a day off?" responded Chris.

"Oh, I can always take a day off. They are pretty lenient with me about those things. What you should have asked was whether I wanted to take a day off. And my answer would have been 'not really.' This is my passion."

The elderly greeter looked around and smiled. "And it reminds me of my Rose. Everywhere I turn here, I see her."

Mr. Gunther sat down across from Chris and gave a big grin. Chris assumed that he must be a morning person. Or maybe the years of being a greeter just made his face always look happy.

"How are you and Mrs. Claire doing? I've been thinking a lot about you guys."

Before Chris answered, he picked up his coffee and took a sip. "We're doing better, I think. What you said and some of what Terry said has made me think."

"Oh, what did Terry tell you?" asked Mr. Gunther.

"To operate as a team. And to be a good teammate. I guess, even in marriage, nobody wants to play with someone who only thinks about themselves."

"That's good advice," replied Mr. Gunther.

"He also said something about the importance of using your resources to make a difference. No, he said to make an 'eternal impact.'"

Mr. Gunther pointed at Chris. "Mr. Terry and Mrs. Mary are the most generous couple I have every met. Our entire staff knows them because of their generosity. And it was their generosity that first caught my attention."

"So they tip well?"

Mr. Gunther laughed. "Well, yes. They do. But they are not just generous with their money. They are generous with their time, words, and anything else they have. They live generously."

Mr. Gunther paused for a few seconds. Chris could tell he was reliving a memory.

"About seven years ago my wife, Rose, fell and injured her hip— right over there." He pointed at the resort entrance. "She was the resort greeter that day and tripped over a piece of luggage. Mr. Terry and Mrs. Mary happened to be out there at the time. They saw everything."

Chris was empathic. "I'm sorry."

"It was one of those rare days when we were short-staffed. Of course, my mind was on Rose and getting her to the hospital, so I recommended that we go without a greeter until the next shift arrived. But then . . ." Mr. Gunther's eyes started to tear up, but he blinked quickly to hold back the tears. "But then, Mr. Terry just stepped in among the staff that had gathered and told me to hurry up and leave.

He said that he and Mrs. Mary would be the greeters until the next shift arrived."

"Wow," uttered Chris.

"Yes. Wow indeed. And they did just that. Needless to say, I will never forget it. Neither will the rest of the resort staff."

"That's amazing," said Chris.

Mr. Gunther continued, "Here's what I know about that rich couple—they give first. Generosity is their priority. And that's true of their money, too. I don't think they would mind my telling you that, financially, they give before they do anything else with the money they make. If you and Mrs. Claire are fighting about money, maybe you should consider chasing after something bigger than just your own financial well-being. Focus on getting your finances right so you can help others. You know, God gives to us so that we can give to others. God designed us to be generous."

Chris smirked. "Terry said something similar."

"Anytime we get closer to God's design for us, we find greater contentment and purpose." Mr. Gunther sat back in his chair, like he was somewhat proud of what he just said.

"So start giving," said Chris.

"It may be a good first step for you and Mrs. Claire."

"Contentment and purpose," Chris said, repeating Mr. Gunther's words.

"What marriage doesn't need that?"

Chris just chuckled and took another sip of his coffee.

Milestone I: Start Giving

We all want our lives to matter. We all want to make a difference in this world. We want God to use us to impact lives on earth and for all eternity. We want to live for something bigger than ourselves.

Generosity does this.

Randy Alcorn penned one of my favorite quotes. It says,

> Giving is a giant lever positioned on the fulcrum of the
> world, allowing us to move mountains in the next world.
> Because we give, eternity will be different—for others and
> for us.[1]

You may be surprised that the first step of your financial journey focuses on generosity. You may wonder why it would be generosity instead of debt or retirement. Both of those goals are important, and we will get to them soon.

But they aren't the most important financial goal.

The reason we start with generosity is simple—the Bible starts with generosity. As God lays out his plan for how we are to manage our money, he starts with giving. The Bible tells us to give generously, save wisely, and live appropriately.

You see, generosity is the foundation upon which real, biblical financial health is experienced. Every money decision we make should be driven by our desire to give generously.

Through giving generously and living with open hands, you will be able to experience the adventure-packed, contentment-filled, kingdom-advancing life God has designed for you.

It's inside of you. You know it. You know that you and your money were meant for something far more than what the world offers. You and your teammate were meant to be a part of something big. God designed you, not to be a hoarder but a conduit through which his generosity flows.

The Four Giving Principles

What does it mean to give? How does it look? These are common questions. You may know intuitively that you should give but not really know anything past that.

The good news is that the Bible shows us what generosity looks like. We serve a generous God, so it is not surprising that we find our generous God guiding us in our giving.

We find four principles of giving woven throughout Scripture.

Principle 1: Giving is to be a priority.

We are given resources so that we can give resources. We are a pass-through—a conduit—for God's generosity to others.

The Bible repeatedly shows us that we are to give our first and our best to him. You may have heard of the term *firstfruits* or *first produce* in conversations about giving. This term is found in the Old Testament. For example, Proverbs 3:9 says, "Honor the LORD with your possessions and with the first produce of your entire harvest."

For the Israelites, this meant that whatever crops or livestock were produced, they were to set aside the first and best of their crops or livestock for God.

What does this mean for us? For most of us, it means that we are to give some of our gross income (the total amount before anything else is taken out) to God. Before taxes, before retirement savings, before debt repayment, and even before bill payments, we give.

This is the opposite of how most give. For most, giving is an afterthought. It's what takes place after all of the needs and wants are taken care of. At the end of the month, they look at their bank account and give what's left.

But this is not what we see in the Bible. In the Bible, giving is a priority.

Principle 2: Giving is to be done proportionately.

This means that those who have more give more, and those who have less give less. Your giving should be proportional to what you have been given.

You probably have heard of the term *tithe. Tithe* means "10 percent." One of the most well-known verses on tithing is Malachi 3:10. It says, "'Bring a full tenth into the storehouse so that there may be food in my house . . . ,' says the LORD of Armies. 'See if I will not open the floodgates of heaven and pour out a blessing for you without measure.'"

So, does this mean that 10 percent is the magic number for giving?

There is much debate surrounding this question, and we won't get into the weeds here. But regardless, it does give a good place to start. Here is my suggestion: If you are not currently giving 10 percent of your gross income, make it your goal to do so. If you are already giving 10 percent, don't let it be your ceiling. For some, giving 10 percent is just a box checked. They don't even think much about it anymore. When this happens, they miss out on how God would work in and through them if they pushed their giving into the sacrificial zone.

Principle 3: Giving is to be done sacrificially.

In God's economy, amount sacrificed always supersedes amount given. God delights in us when we give, not out of abundance but out of sacrifice.

When King David went to offer God a sacrifice, a man tried to give him land and animals at no cost. In 2 Samuel 24:24, we read King David's response: "No, I insist on buying it from you for a price, for I will not offer to the LORD my God burnt offerings that cost me nothing."

He knew that God would find greater delight in an offering that cost him something.

To give sacrificially means that giving should create some level of discomfort. It means that we will forego something else. The thought that should cross your mind when you give is not, "Well, I don't really need it" but "This means that I will not be able to do or buy what I desire."

For those who may find themselves in a financially difficult situation, where you think that giving is just not an option, let me offer these thoughts:

God does not provide an exclusion clause for giving.

God delights in those who obey when obedience is not convenient.

Don't let a bad financial decision from the past cause you to make another bad financial decision. Remember, God tells us to give. And those whose giving is most celebrated in the Bible are those who gave when it wasn't easy.

You may think that the little you are able to give is just not worth it. If this is you, remember that we serve a God of multiplication. He is the one who took a couple of fish and a few loaves of bread and fed the five thousand.

He can do the same with what you give. God can use your small gift to make an eternal difference.

Principle: 4: Giving is to be done cheerfully.

Second Corinthians 9:7 says, "Each person should do as he has decided in his heart—not reluctantly or out of compulsion, since God loves a cheerful giver."

Have you ever received a gift where the person made sure to point out how much it cost them? It's like they weren't happy to give you the gift. Perhaps you even told them to keep the gift. Or, if you did keep it, the joy was gone.

While God delights in sacrificial giving, he does not delight in miserable giving. At times the principles of sacrificial giving and cheerful giving may seem to contradict each other. How can you give out of discomfort and still be happy?

God shows us how.

Isaiah 53:10 reads, "Yet the LORD was pleased to crush him severely. When you make him a guilt offering he will see his seed, he will prolong his days, and by his hand the LORD's pleasure will be accomplished."

That first "him" is Jesus. God found pleasure in the crushing, or the crucifixion, of his Son. But how? How can God find delight in the midst of the pain?

He focused on eternity.

He focused on the unfathomable, lasting outcome that would result from the crushing of Jesus; his seed, us, will be with him for all eternity.

And that is how you find happiness in the midst of sacrifice. Focus on the eternal ramifications.

Our Generous God

God did not just tell us how to give. He showed us. He leads us in our giving.

Think about it.

God gave us his first and his best. Giving was a priority.

God owns everything. Therefore, he gave to an extent no one else could give. He gave proportionately.

God allowed his Son to be sacrificed for the forgiveness of our sins. He gave sacrificially.

And yet he found pleasure in the sacrifice because of the eternal rewards. God was a cheerful giver.

We don't serve a God who just talks about generosity; he leads us in it.

The Takeoff

Maybe the idea of giving away a portion of your income makes you nervous. Or maybe you just can't see how you can survive without using all of your income.

If this is you, you are not alone. I've heard these concerns from many people. They know that they *should* give; they just can't imagine how they *could*.

For those who are afraid or hesitant to give, I recommend The Takeoff. The Takeoff is a guide to help you go from giving nothing to giving 10 percent over 12 months.

Here is how it looks:

- Months 1–3: Give 1 percent of gross income to your local church.
- Months 4–6: Give 3 percent of gross income to your local church.
- Months 7–9: Give 5 percent of gross income to your local church.
- Months 10–11: Give 7 percent of gross income to your local church.
- Month 12: Give 10 percent of gross income to your local church.

And throughout this year, pray that God will develop in you a heart that trusts him with your money.

What I love about The Takeoff is that once a person begins to taste a generous lifestyle, particularly in months 1–3, they realize that giving is more doable than they thought, and the excitement of being a part of something big and eternal motivates them to give more. This is a result of God's designing us to live generously.

The most difficult part is trusting God with that first step, going from zero to something. But it is a step worth taking.

Start Giving

If you are a believer in Jesus, you have been forgiven much. The outcome of this should be love that flows into generosity. We are generous because God has been so generous to us.

Where should you start giving? Your local church should be the first place. The local church is God's primary strategy to make his name known in your community and around the world. So start there.

Live generously. Be a part of God's mission. God designed you for this. Giving takes faith and intentionality. Decide to live generously. If you've never given, consider The Takeoff. Remember, generosity is the foundation upon which real, biblical financial health is found. Generosity is the "why" behind the pursuit of financial health.

Your Marriage Challenges

Day 8 Marriage Challenge: *Start giving.* Real, biblical financial health starts with generosity. If you have never given, start with just 1 percent of your gross income and try to get to 10 percent. Let your local church be your first place of giving. Make your first gift today.

Day 9 Marriage Challenge: *Have a conversation about generosity.* Use these conversation starters:

1. Who is the most generous person you know? What characteristics do they display?

2. When was the last time you helped someone in need? How did it make you feel? Why?

3. Why is your local church vital to your community? What has God accomplished through your local church?

CHAPTER 6

Just in Case

Another perfect day.

"It makes you just want to pack up everything and move down here," said Claire.

"I'm not opposed to it," replied Chris with a grin. "Let's just stay right here. I'm probably not going to have a job soon in Charlotte anyway."

"Stop it," said Claire.

They were lying out on the lounge chairs surrounding the pool. Chris and Claire had just finished discussing the comments Mr. Gunther made at breakfast. They agreed that generosity needed to be a priority. They wanted their marriage and their money to be about something more significant than the constant pursuit of bigger and better. In fact, Mary had already sent a gift to their church, Christ Community, using her phone. They figured it was a good start.

As they lay there, Chris and Claire heard a familiar voice.

"So what are the repairs?" And then after a few seconds. "Man, that's great. I can't wait to hear about it later."

It was Terry. He was talking on his phone. He continued, "Okay. Be sure to take care of her. Don't charge her anything. Talk to you later." Terry hung up the phone.

Terry would have walked right by Chris and Claire had Claire not called out his name.

"Terry!" she yelled.

Terry stopped right in front of the couple.

"Oh, hey! How are you guys doing today? You both are looking pretty relaxed."

"We are. Were you talking to your shop back in Chicago?" asked Chris.

"I was," replied Terry.

"Sounds like you are giving away free car repairs. Is there a coupon out for that? If so, I'll take two!" joked Chris.

Terry laughed. "Unfortunately not. There was just a lady who needed her car repaired badly, but she couldn't afford it. So we're just doing the repairs for free. We do that on occasion." Terry paused and smiled. "Just don't tell anybody. We can't do it for everyone. I do have employees to pay."

Chris and Claire were now laughing, but it came to an abrupt stop with Terry's next comment.

"It's amazing how many people do not have enough money saved for a small emergency, like a car repair. Of course, I can empathize. I was one of them. If this lady had $1,500 or so in an emergency fund, she wouldn't have to stress over her car like she is now. Things would still be tight for her, but not this tight. I hope that after she gets her car back, she'll start saving some money."

Chris and Claire subtly looked at each other. They hadn't thought about an emergency fund. But neither of them was going to admit that to Terry.

"Well, honeymooners, my wife is somewhere out there on that beach, so I'm off to find her. See you guys later." He gave a quick wave and put the phone in his pocket.

"See you later, Terry," said Chris.

After Terry walked away, Chris looked at Claire; this time it wasn't subtle. "I'm going to start taking a few notes. I think we can both learn a lot from this couple."

Claire nodded in agreement. "I guess if we ever got in a bind, we could ask my parents for help." Claire smirked. She knew Chris wouldn't like that thought.

Chris quickly took out his phone and typed some quick notes:

> 1. *Start giving.*
> 2. *$1,500 minor emergency fund.*

He then set his phone down on a beach towel next to his chair, let out an audible sigh, and listened to the waves hit the surf.

"Yes, this wouldn't be too bad of a place to live."

Milestone 2: Save $1,500 for a Minor Emergency

Instant gratification.

It has changed our perception. Time feels different than it used to. Waiting a week feels like waiting a month. Waiting a month feels like, well, waiting an eternity.

We live in a world where we can get what we want when we want it. Right now I can open an app on my phone, purchase a television, and have it delivered to my house within an hour. If I want to watch a movie, I can open another app and pick from a huge selection of movies to view right now. And if I need an answer to a question, I can simply open up my web browser and "Google it."

Credit cards allow us to make purchases, not just right away but when we don't even have the actual money to purchase it. We don't have to wait on accumulating enough cash to make the purchase.

Saving money runs against instant gratification. Maybe this is one of the reasons we struggle to do it. Only 41 percent of adults in America have enough saved to cover an emergency costing $500 to $1,000. That means six out of ten adults don't even have $500 in savings.[1]

That's scary.

You and your teammate don't need to be one of those six.

The Bible and Savings

Why do we save?

To give.

Seriously.

Since generosity is our financial priority, making sure we have enough for unforeseen financial emergencies and retirement protects that priority. When we have not planned well for emergencies and retirement, our ability to live generously is hindered. We don't set aside money just to have piles of cash on hand. We save so that when an unanticipated cost hits, we can take care of it and keep giving.

Does saving help reduce financial stress? Absolutely. But it also allows us to experience the generous life God designed us to live.

We save to give.

The Bible speaks to the importance of preparing for the future in a very clear way. In the book of Proverbs, we find King Solomon using the ant as an example for how to save.

> Go to the ant, you slacker! Observe its ways and become
> wise. Without leader, administrator, or ruler, it prepares its
> provisions in summer; it gathers its food during harvest.
> (Prov. 6:6–8)

Later in Proverbs, King Solomon points out the wisdom of saving versus constantly spending every dollar we receive.

> Precious treasure and oil are in the dwelling of a wise per-
> son, but a fool consumes them. (Prov. 21:20)

The Bible teaches us that we are wise to save. There are seasons of abundance and seasons of scarcity. We are to take advantage when there is abundance, setting aside money for the future. Spending every penny will eventually harm us because there will be seasons of scarcity when our income isn't where we want it to be but our expenses still exist.

And like the ant we can protect our generosity and ourselves by persistently saving. Saving for the future is not a single event. For most of us, it will happen over time as we regularly set aside money in our savings and retirement accounts. Saving needs to be a habit.

Your Minor Emergency Fund

At some point you are going to get hit with an unexpected expense. I don't know when, but it's coming. A tire will go flat. Your hot water heater will leak. Your air conditioner will stop cooling the house. In fact, you were probably hit with one or more unexpected expenses just this past year. These expenses are really frustrating but also really normal. They are minor emergencies.

If you don't have money set aside for these expenses, you and your teammate will probably resort to using credit cards, which leads to more debt. That means these expenses only get more expensive, increase your stress, and reduce your giving.

There is a better way.

You need a minor emergency fund.

After you start giving, this is your next financial step. Emergency funds are critical for anyone's financial health.

A minor emergency fund is a lump of money set aside to cover the normal, unplanned expenses that hit most of us. For this fund you need to have a minimum of $1,500. That amount should be enough to take care of small car repairs, house repairs, and minor medical expenses.

Where do you put your minor emergency fund? The minor emergency fund can be placed in a free checking account at your local bank. These accounts do not require a minimum balance, and they usually come with a debit card.

But don't use it for everyday purchases. Have another account for that.

Use your minor emergency fund only when you get hit with an unanticipated expense. That's what it is there for.

Finding Your $1,500

You and your teammate may be thinking there is no way you can save $1,500. Many have that same thought, as indicated by our national saving statistics.

But you can do it. Like any financial goal, you have to be patient but persistent. Here are some suggestions on how to jump-start your minor emergency fund:

1. Sell Some Stuff

Like most of us, you probably have a few items in your house that have not been used in a few years. This is a pretty good indication that you don't really need those items. So make a few bucks by selling them. There are several online platforms that allow you to sell your stuff. As an example, our community has a Buy/Sell page on Facebook. This page has become our go-to for items my wife and I want to sell.

2. Get a Gig

There are a several ways to earn extra income these days. Drive for Uber. Sell homemade products on Etsy. If you have the know-how, do graphics or website development on the side. I have a friend who walks dogs for extra income. Of course, if your company offers overtime, pick up a few hours. The opportunities to earn extra income are seemingly endless. Try one or two.

3. Avoid Restaurants

Americans eat out a lot. You're probably spending more money eating out than you realize. So cut out restaurants for a while and save a few bucks by making your own food at home. Place the money you would pay at a restaurant in your minor emergency fund account.

4. Renegotiate Rates

When was the last time you contacted your cable, Internet, or cell phone service provider to talk rates? These types of service companies offer discounts on a regular basis. Make sure you are taking advantage of them. Also, customer service representatives often have the ability to reduce your rate, even when a discount is not advertised. So talk to them about a rate reduction.

5. Budget

Look, I get it. You can't stand the thought of budgeting. But budgeting can help you identify where you are overspending. You may find out that your $1,500 was hiding right under a few avoidable expenses. Get your expenditures in line with your income, and try to set aside money for savings each month.

You can get to $1,500 faster than you think. Get creative and strategic. Find ways to temporarily increase your income while decreasing expenditures. The combined effort will leave you with a $1,500 minor emergency fund in no time.

Focus on $1,500

You and your teammate are probably feeling overwhelmed with all the financial decisions you need to make. You feel like you are so far behind that you will never catch up. And you want to solve all of your problems today.

Right now, focus on the $1,500.

Remember, if you have $1,500 set aside for emergencies, you are more financially stable than the majority of adults in America. If you don't have a minor emergency fund set up, a relatively small expense can send your world into a tailspin and erode any progress you have made in other areas of your finances.

I hope the unanticipated expense is not in your near future, but there is no way I can know that. And neither can you.

It sounds simple, but a minor emergency fund is crucial. And if you have one, you have accomplished something significant. You haven't completely arrived financially, but you are off to a great start.

Your Marriage Challenges

Day 10 Marriage Challenge: *Give something away.* Find something in your house that you haven't used in a while. Next, give it to someone you know would want it, or donate the item. But please be sure to check with your spouse first. Just trust me on this one.

Day 11 Marriage Challenge: *Have a conversation about your minor emergency fund.* Use these marriage and money conversation starters:

1. What minor unplanned expense ($1,500 or less) did you experience this past year?

2. If you were to predict your next minor emergency, what do you think it would be?

3. How can you find $1,500 to set aside, and where should you put it?

CHAPTER 7

Free Money

After being out on the pool deck for a few hours, Chris and Claire decided to go inside. Walking past the resort business offices, they saw what appeared to be a small celebration. The room was packed with staff members.

A loud applause erupted among the gathering, and members began to trickle out of the office area. Chris stopped one of the staff members to ask what the celebration was about.

"Oh, Jeremiah, one of our staff members is retiring at the end of the week. So we thought we'd throw him a surprise retirement party. Great guy. He'll be missed."

Chris had another unfiltered moment. "Yikes. I hope he has enough money to make it."

"What do you mean?" asked the staff member.

Chris immediately wished he had not made that comment. He could not think of a way to answer the question without potentially offending the staff member. So he decided to be blunt.

"I mean, I know how some of these positions probably don't pay enough to set aside anything significant for retirement." Chris grimaced. This wasn't his finest moment.

The staff member put his hand on Chris's shoulder. "First of all, the resort does a good job on pay. Second, the resort has provided a retirement contribution match since 1980. And it is a pretty large match. Jeremiah has been taking advantage of that match since 1980. So he is doing alright. The resort takes care of their employees. We are a team."

Chris was embarrassed. The look on Claire's face indicated that she was as well. It was another foot-in-mouth situation. He was sure he would hear about it later. But he was curious about the match and how it helped set people up for retirement. He and Claire had not put anything toward retirement yet.

"So, tell me a little more about this match."

"Well, when we put money toward our 401(k), The Miami Palms Resort matches that money up to a certain point. It helps us accumulate more for retirement."

"That's great."

The staff member continued, "You see, the key to saving up enough for retirement, like Jeremiah did, is to start early. If you take advantage of a match early, you can end up with a lot of money. You look pretty young. If your employer offers a match, take it."

Chris was not expecting to take retirement advice from a staff person at a resort. But then again, there was really nothing about this trip that seemed normal any longer.

The staff member said, "Look, I'm serious. Our resort makes sure that we are setting aside money for retirement. So we're lucky in that regard. Most don't think about retirement until it's too late. Don't be one of those people."

Just then, Terry and Mary walked by.

"Hey, I found my wife!" Terry joked.

The staff member immediately recognized the rich couple. "How are you doing today, Mr. Terry and Mrs. Mary? Is there anything I can help you with?"

"No thank you. That's very kind," replied Mary.

"We were just talking about retirement and employer matches," said Chris. "Does Terry's Auto Shop offer a match?"

Terry beamed. "Absolutely. We actually took a cue from how this resort takes care of its employees. I want all of my employees to be retirement ready. And, Chris, if your company offers a match, be sure to get it."

"Of course. I will," responded Chris.

Terry and Mary walked away. The staff member shook Chris's and Claire's hands and walked away as well.

"Well, I didn't expect that conversation," Chris said as he pulled out his phone.

"Can you not stick your foot in your mouth so much?" Claire said with a light snicker.

"I know. I know. I know."

Chris typed in phone:

> *3. Get employer match.*

Milestone 3: Max Out Your 401(k) or 403(b) Match

Imagine that today is the first day at your new job. You walk through the front glass doors and into the office building, excited but somewhat nervous. To get this job, you traveled a difficult and tiring road. You don't want to mess it up.

One of your first meetings is with the human resources department. You sit down at the desk, and they place a stack of papers in front of you.

The lady with whom you meet is nice enough. She shares with you the benefits package you will receive. The benefits are good, and you are grateful for that.

She concludes the meeting by discussing the company's retirement savings plan. She mentions this thing called a "match" and hands over more paperwork to fill out. Fortunately, she doesn't need it immediately. You can take it home and think about it.

You walk out of the office, still thinking about the retirement savings plan. Should you sign up? And what about this match? Is it the right step for you now? Should you even care about retirement? There are so many years between now and retirement.

Really? Retirement?

I know. Retirement seems far off for you and your teammate. But that is exactly why you should care. Far away from retirement is exactly when you want to start saving.

Here is a formula worth remembering:

A little bit of money + A lot of time = A lot of money

Time will fly. Ask anyone older than you. Before you know it, you will be packing up your office. There will be a few balloons still lingering on the ceiling from your retirement celebration. And as you take one last look around your now bare office, your emotions are mixed. You are somewhat excited, somewhat sad, and somewhat nervous.

Ready or not, retirement, here you come.

At this point, there are no do-overs. For better or worse, you will reap the financial fruit of your preparation.

Preparing for retirement is preparing for future generosity. Your ability to live with open hands in the future may depend on how well you plan today.

Your retirement preparation, or lack of preparation, can also impact your children's future generosity. Adult children often pay the price for parents who did not plan well.

So, yes, when you are young is the perfect time to take retirement seriously.

And it starts with an understanding of compounding.

Compounding

Compounding. You may have heard that term before. What is compounding, and why is it so important?

We're going to start with a little math. Don't worry; I won't get too carried away with the numbers.

Let's say you invested $10 and over the course of a year, you earned a 10 percent return, meaning that the amount you invested grew by 10 percent. For that year, you would have earned $1 ($10 x 10%). So now you have $11 ($10+$1).

Let's say that the next year, you earn another 10 percent on your investment. Because you started the second year with $11 and not $10 like the year prior, you earn $11x10% = $1.10. So after two years you have $12.10.

Compounding is earning money on your earned money. Compounding is not as much about addition as it is multiplication.

Each year, your increase is not just based on the original amount invested (in our example, the $10) but the total amount of the original investment and whatever gains you had.

Why is this important? Well, over time, you can see significant growth in your investments.

Consider this. What do you think would happen if a sixteen-year-old decided to set aside $2,000 for three years (a total of $6,000 in three years) in a retirement account and simply achieved the same return as the S&P 500 (a performance indicator for the U.S. stock market) from 1967 to 2016?

Age	Contribution	S&P Return	Growth
16	$2,000.00	23.80%	$2,476.00
17	$2,000.00	10.81%	$4,743.66
18	$2,000.00	−8.24%	$6,352.78
19	$0.00	3.56%	$6,578.94
20	$0.00	14.22%	$7,514.46
21	$0.00	18.76%	$8,924.18
22	$0.00	−14.31%	$7,647.13
23	$0.00	−25.90%	$5,666.52
24	$0.00	37.00%	$7,763.13
25	$0.00	23.83%	$9,613.09
26	$0.00	−6.98%	$8,942.09
27	$0.00	6.51%	$9,524.22
28	$0.00	18.52%	$11,288.11
29	$0.00	31.74%	$14,870.96
30	$0.00	−4.70	$14,172.02
31	$0.00	20.42%	$17,065.95
32	$0.00	22.34%	$20,878.48
33	$0.00	6.15%	$22,162.51
34	$0.00	31.24%	$29,086.08
35	$0.00	18.49%	$34,464.09
36	$0.00	5.81%	$36,466.45
37	$0.00	16.54%	$42,498.01
38	$0.00	31.48%	$55,876.38
39	$0.00	−3.06%	$54,166.56
40	$0.00	30.23%	$70,541.11
41	$0.00	7.49%	$75,824.64
42	$0.00	9.97%	$83,384.36
43	$0.00	1.33%	$84,493.37
44	$0.00	37.20%	$115,924.90
45	$0.00	22.68%	$142,216.67
46	$0.00	33.10%	$189,290.39
47	$0.00	28.34%	$242,935.29
48	$0.00	20.89%	$293,684.47
49	$0.00	−9.03%	$267,164.76
50	$0.00	−11.85%	$235,505.74
51	$0.00	−21.97%	$183,765.13
52	$0.00	28.36%	$235,880.92
53	$0.00	10.74%	$261,214.53
54	$0.00	4.83%	$273,831.19
55	$0.00	15.61%	$316,576.24
56	$0.00	5.48%	$333,924.62
57	$0.00	−36.55%	$211,875.17
58	$0.00	25.94%	$266,835.59
59	$0.00	14.82%	$306,380.62
60	$0.00	2.10%	$312,814.61
61	$0.00	15.89%	$362,520.86
62	$0.00	32.15%	$479,071.31
63	$0.00	13.52%	$543,841.75
64	$0.00	1.36%	$551,346.77
65	$0.00	11.74%	**$616,074.88**

Even if they did not invest any more money, that $6,000 would have turned into more than $600,000. That's right. More than $600,000.

How? Compounding.

Now, don't we all regret spending our summer money on pizza and movies?

With compounding, a little bit of money plus a long period of time can equal a lot of money.

So when it comes to your retirement, start saving as soon as possible to take full advantage of compounding. And for some, this starts with our company's retirement savings plan.

401(k) / 403(b)

A 401(k) is a retirement savings plan that you get through your employer. It's what we call an employer-sponsored plan, meaning that if you don't work for that particular company, you cannot access the plan. If you work for a nonprofit, it's called a 403(b). If you work for the government, it's called a 457(b). There are some differences between these plans, but they are all similar.

With these plans, you are able to take a portion of your gross (before taxes) income from your paycheck and put it into the plan. Therefore, you don't pay taxes on this part of your income right away.

Why is this important? Well, it allows more money to go into the plan for your future retirement and reduces your taxable income for that year. Now this does not mean that you completely avoid taxes. You do pay ordinary income taxes when you take the money out. But hopefully this only happens in your retirement years, when income and the taxes you pay on it tend to be low anyway.

Once the money is in the plan, you typically choose one of the investment options provided by the plan. The goal is to grow your money in the plan.

For the 401(k) and 403(b), you can take the money out without any penalties once you turn 59 ½ years of age. If you take it out prior to that, there is a 10 percent penalty in addition to income taxes. For the government plans, there is no penalty, but you do have to pay income taxes on it.

Some employers are now offering a Roth 401(k) or Roth 403(b). These plans require you to contribute after-tax dollars. However, you get to withdraw the income tax-free without penalty at age 59 ½. If you withdraw early, a penalty often applies. So, like the traditional 401(k), plan on keeping the money in there until retirement.

So, what should you do if your job gives you access to an employer-sponsored plan like a 401(k), 403(b), or 457(b)?

If they offer an employee match, jump in.

Employer Match

Some organizations offer what's called a "match." The concept is fairly simple. The organization agrees to match some or all of your contribution into their retirement savings plan, up to a certain percentage.

Let's say that your company offers a 3 percent, dollar for dollar, match. This means that whatever you contribute to the retirement saving plan, they will match your contribution, up to 3 percent of your gross income. So if your salary is $50,000 and you contribute $1,500 (3%), they will place an additional $1,500 into your retirement plan. That's a 100 percent return on your investment!

Consider a second example. Let's say your company matches $0.50 on every dollar you contribute up to 5 percent. If your salary is still $50,000 and you contribute 5 percent ($2,500) of your gross income, your company will contribute an additional $1,250. That's a 50 percent return on your investment!

Incredible. Ensuring you get your company match is probably one of the best financial investments you can make. Where else would you get that type of return on your money?

But remember, the only way you can get the company's match is to contribute to the plan yourself. If you don't contribute, they don't contribute. And if you contribute below the maximum match, the company will only match the amount you contribute. It's still a good deal, but you are leaving money on the table.

What Is Vesting?

Vesting answers the question, "When do I get to keep my company match?" To be clear, you immediately own any money *you* put into your retirement savings plan. Your money is your money.

But this is not always the case with the money your company contributes. In order to encourage employees to stay longer, some companies gradually transfer ownership of their retirement contributions to employees. How companies do this will vary.

One company may transfer 25 percent ownership each year to the employee. Another company may transfer 100 percent of the ownership on year three. And another company may give employees immediate ownership.

Check with your human resources area to determine what your company's vesting schedule looks like. "Fully vested" means you have reached the point where you have full ownership on the company's contributions.

Why Get the Match Now?

Take advantage of your company match now.

You probably notice that the company match hits pretty early in the Milestone sequence. Start giving, set aside $1,500, and then get your employer match, if available.

For a variety of reasons, some employees decide to hold off on maxing out their employer's match. So, why should you almost always invest the maximum amount your employer will match?

1. If you don't, you miss a huge opportunity. Your employer's match may not seem that significant to you. You wonder how such a small percentage can really make a difference anyway. It can. In fact, over time, it can make a huge difference. This is the beauty of compounding.

2. You will barely miss it. I've seen it happen over and over again—an employee says there is no way they can afford to contribute 2.5 percent of their salary, or whatever the maximum match amount is. But then they give it a shot. And they realize that the net amount per paycheck wasn't nearly as much as they thought. Remember, the contributions are based on your gross salary. Contributions to a 401(k) and 403(b) are pretax. So the impact to your budget is 2.5 percent minus taxes. I have heard it said by many, "I barely miss it."

3. It's your money. It's a benefit that is given to you because of your employment. It is part of your employment package. It is your money for the taking. To opt out means that you leave money on the table, money that can have a significant impact on your future retirement. Skipping out on your match is literally declining money.

How should you invest the money? Let me provide a suggestion if you are just starting out and know little about investing. Most employer-sponsored plans have target funds. Target funds adjust the investments within the fund according to your anticipated retirement year. For example, you may have the option to invest in Target Fund 2045. This means that fund selects investments they deem suitable for someone looking to retire in the year 2045. The further out your retirement, the more aggressively they invest. The closer you are to the retirement year, the more conservative the investment choices. All you have to do is select the fund that aligns with your anticipated retirement year.

Are target funds perfect? No. They are not silver bullets. But they can be a good place to start if you have little investment knowledge or experience.

Don't Miss Out

The opportunity cost is too great not to take advantage of your company match, even before paying off debt, so contribute whatever it takes to get the full match there.

Often the match is referred to as "free money." But it can also be considered "earned money." You have access to it because of your work. A match is a benefit you earned. So go ahead and take it. You earned it.

I know that not all organizations provide a match. But if your company does, don't miss out on this incredible opportunity.

Remember the power of compounding. A little bit of money over a long period of time can generate a lot of money for you and your teammate's retirement.

If your employer does not offer a match, that's okay. Hold off on putting money into your retirement until you've reached Milestone 5.

Your Money Challenges

Day 12 Marriage Challenge: *Surprise someone together.* Both of you buy a gift card. It doesn't have to be much. And then give them to two people before you leave the store, hopefully to someone you've never met.

Day 13 Marriage Challenge: *Talk about retirement.* Use these marriage and money conversation starters:

1. What did you think about the chart that showed $6,000 turning into $600,000?

2. Do you have any family members or friends who are financially struggling during their retirement years? What is their story?

3. Does your company offer a match? If so, what is the match, and what steps do you need to take to get it?

CHAPTER 8

Crushing Your Debt

"You know, before we got here, I thought more money would lead to a greater fulfillment in life. After meeting the rich couple, I've realized that I believed a lie. They do have a lot, and they do seem to be satisfied. But Mr. Gunther is a greeter, and yet he seems to be just as content as they are. Money doesn't get you there. Mission does. You have to live for something bigger than yourself, and money can be a piece of that, through generosity."

Chris looked across the table to see what Claire thought of his words. He could tell she was listening but thinking at the same time. So his eyes shifted to the dinner plate in front of him, and he continued moving forward with his stream of consciousness.

"I mean, who really cares if you have all the money in the world if you have no significant purpose for it? Chasing more stuff will make you happy for a minute, but then that happiness will be gone, and all you will want is more. It's just like that new car smell—intoxicating at first, but it goes away. And when it leaves, your car smells like, well, you. And you don't like the smell of you, so you go to get another new-smelling car to cover up your reality. Your self-focused, purpose-lacking reality."

He looked up at Claire. Her eyes were wide open, staring at Chris. "Well, that's kind of depressing. Great dinner conversation, honey." They both laughed.

"Sorry about that," said Chris.

Claire smiled. "That's okay. In a weird way, you actually make sense. Which makes me regret my debt. I didn't think it was a big deal before, but now I realize that my debt will get in the way of using our money for more meaningful purposes."

"What do you mean?" asked Chris.

"Well, whether we want to or not, we're going to have to pay our bills. When we get that notice in the mail that says we owe them a monthly payment for my debt, we have to pay it. Whatever the bill is, we can't use it for something else. That money is already committed. Debt is a generosity killer."

"Yup. *Debt is a generosity killer.*" He looked at Claire. Her slight frown made clear that she had been hit by a sense of regret and guilt.

"Look, Claire, I'm not going to say that I'm okay with all the debt. That would be a lie. But what I will say is that what is done is done. And instead of dwelling on past decisions, we should focus on how to move forward. Because we can move forward. This debt is not the end of us. It's not even the end of our generosity. We're still going to give. We need to make it our priority. But let's make it a goal to get rid of our debt so that we can live even more generously."

Chris's words were filled with passion. Claire appreciated this. And he was right. Dwelling on the past would never move them forward. Sure, they could learn from their past financial mistakes. But it was up to them not to let their financial past define their financial future. They had two options—self-loathing or chasing after God's design for their money.

Softly but firmly, Claire spoke, "We have to get rid of our debt. Not just for the sake of us, but for the sake of those lives God can change by using the money that's currently committed to debt repayment."

"Yes!" Chris said as he banged his fist on the table. The noise drew the attention of other dinner tables.

"Please don't do that," requested Claire.

"Right. Sorry." Then he repeated Terry's words, "Eternal impact."

Claire nodded her head in agreement. "It's worth chasing. Seems a lot more compelling than chasing a new-car smell."

"Now you see what I mean!" Chris said with a big smile. He took out his phone and typed another note:

4. Get rid of debt.

"Do you sense that?" asked Chris.

"What?" responded Claire, not really sure she wanted to know the answer.

"Oneness." Chris was grinning from cheek to cheek.

Claire just smirked, rolled her eyes, and said, "Wow, you're cheesy."

Milestone 4: Pay Off All Debt Except Your Mortgage

One of the most concerning areas of Americans' personal finances is debt.

Why do we get into loads of debt? The answer varies. For some, it's due to a lack of understanding about debt and its consequences. For others, it can be traced back to a lack of self-esteem, buying things in hopes that they will feel better about themselves. For others, it's due to an unforeseen emergency that could not be covered by savings. And for some, it's because they did not search out alternative options for their situation. They just went with the easiest option, swiping their credit card.

But for all, the result is the same—the burden of debt.

Debt can take a big toll on us. It can increase our stress and has even been linked to depression and a decreased confidence in one's ability to manage their money.

Of course, there are also financial ramifications. Those Americans that have credit card debt average around a $16,000 balance. Those with automobile loans average approximately $29,000 in car loans. And Americans with student loan debt average about $46,000 in student loan debt.[1]

We are a nation of people strapped with debt.

The Bible and Debt

The Bible speaks to the issue of debt. Here is a summary:

1. Be cautious about going into debt.
2. If you do go into debt, you will be burdened.
3. Even though you hate the burden, you must still pay your bills.

Proverbs 22:26–27 says, "Don't be one of those who enter agreements, who put up security for loans. If you have nothing with which to pay, even your bed will be taken from you."

While the Bible does not identify debt as a sin, God does warn us about it. The Bible tells us to be cautious about diving into debt. We are to scrutinize each purchase decision. Is the purchase wise? Does it fit within the budget? For the most part, it is wise to avoid debt. Consider your other options before taking the easy, debt-laden route.

Here's why: "The rich rule over the poor, and the borrower is a slave to the lender." That's Proverbs 22:7.

Let's say you received $100 for some side work. You and your spouse are considering how to spend that $100. You want to use it for a nice date. Your spouse wants to use it to decorate the home. Both of you agree that you could use the money to purchase food for the local homeless shelter.

As you discuss the possibilities, you begin to thumb through the mail. You come across a credit card bill and open it up. The amount due reads $100.

What do you do?

You stop the conversation and pay the bill. Why? Because you are a slave to the lender. You are obligated to pay them back, interest and all, whether you want to or not.

And if you decide not to repay them, *"even your bed will be taken from you."* Often, your lender has the ability to take the stuff you purchase back. This is called repossession. Even if they don't repossess the purchase, they can ruin your credit by reporting the missing payments to the credit bureaus.

Inevitably, being debt-laden will frustrate you. It will cause stress. I don't know anybody who says, "I love paying my lender back." Instead, you will see the scenario as burdensome and will want it to end as soon as possible. Nobody enjoys being a slave to the lender.

But we still have to pay our bills.

Psalm 37:21 says, "The wicked person borrows and does not repay, but the righteous one is gracious and giving."

No matter how burdensome and frustrating it may be for you to repay your lender, you must do it. According to God, it is *wicked* not to meet your debt obligations. Avoiding bills should not be an option for Christians. I don't know about you, but *wicked* is not a word I want attached to my name.

The Bible is clear—be cautious about going into debt. If you do go into debt, you will be burdened. And even though you hate the burden, you must still pay your bills.

Now let's look at some of the damaging effects of debt.

The Downside of Debt

If you have debt, you already feel its effects. You feel the burden and stress attached to it. There may have been a moment of happiness when the initial purchase was made, but more than likely that happiness has since faded and maybe even turned into regret.

Why is debt so dangerous? Why is it so bad for us? Let's consider six reasons for this.

The high interest rates. This is especially true for credit cards. Credit card interest rates can easily climb above 20 percent.

Imagine that you decided to purchase new furniture for your house. The total cost was $5,000. You didn't have the money to cover the purchase so you used your credit card with a 21 percent interest rate. The minimum payment was $100, which is all you ever plan to pay. At this pace, it will take you ten years to pay off that balance, and you will have paid almost $7,000 in interest. Your $5,000 purchase becomes a $12,000 purchase.

You better really like that sofa.

The minimum payments. Part of the issue you are facing in the prior example is the low minimum payment. I know it seems odd to say that a low payment is dangerous, but it is. For credit cards, the minimum payment tends to run anywhere between 1 percent and 3 percent of the balance. These low minimum payments may seem nice at first. They make you feel like you can afford to buy more. However, what they are doing is stretching out the life of your debt so that the credit card company can collect more and more interest. Sneaky, right?

Debt is often on a depreciating item. The word *depreciate* means "to go down in value." Most purchases we make—other than our house and retirement investments—depreciate over time.

Using debt to buy items that depreciate is a problem because you often find yourself in a place where the debt is greater than the value of the purchased item.

In other words, you are upside down on that item. If you hit a financially difficult time, you cannot sell the item and repay the debt.

Consider the $5,000 furniture purchase. Within a few months, you will not be able to sell the furniture for the amount needed to pay off your debt on the furniture. In fact, if you just make the minimum payment, you will probably need to buy new furniture before you have paid off the debt on the old furniture.

Debt is a symptom of something more significant. "Why do I really want to buy this item that I cannot afford?" This is a question everyone should ask prior to taking on debt. Sometimes we make purchases in an attempt to satisfy a yearning that the purchase will never fulfill.

For example, you may think that by purchasing clothes you can't afford, you will boost your self-esteem. And, for a moment, you may. But that boost in self-esteem is temporal. And when the boost subsides, all you have left is disappointment and debt.

Debt was a symptom of something more significant. Debt was a symptom of an internal struggle that material items will never alleviate.

Debt hurts your future. In an upcoming chapter, we are going to discuss how to plan for a financially sound retirement. Maintaining debt will hurt your ability to do this.

Debt hinders generosity. Debt limits your ability to live and give like God designed you to do. You cannot live with totally open hands while still enslaved to the burden of debt. You can't give as freely as you desire because you are obligated to make your debt payments.

Imagine what your generosity could look like if you didn't have credit card debt, student loans, car loans, or even a mortgage. It's an exciting thought.

Debt is a generosity killer.

So let's destroy it.

You Aren't What You Drive

I received a phone call from a friend with a financial question. He's the kind of guy who drives his cars until the engine no longer turns. An odometer reading 200,000 miles is nothing to him. If anyone gets his money's worth out of a car, it's my friend.

So my friend asked me, "Art, I think I've found a good deal on a brand-new car. What do you think?"

My response was brief but to the point—"Don't do it." Internally, I wanted to tell him to go for it. But I couldn't. Buying a new car rarely makes financial sense.

The reason for this is that cars depreciate over time. To depreciate means to go down in value.

The average cost of a new car in 2017 was $35,870.[2] But to simplify the numbers, let's say you bought a new car for $30,000. The moment you drive off the car lot, you can expect your new car to depreciate by about 10 percent, or $3,000. After the first year, your car probably has gone down in value by about 25 percent, or $7,500. In only three years, the value of your car has dropped by 46 percent, or $13,800.[3]

That's a big chunk of money.

Usually by this point, the mileage is still low and the car can be driven for many more years. So if you buy a three-year-old car, you will pay much less but still have an automobile that is in good shape.

Since the greatest depreciation occurs in the first few years of a car's life, why not let someone else take the new-car hit?

I understand the allure of a new car; it looks and smells so good. But buying a new car is a big waste of money.

The trust factor for purchasing a quality used car has greatly improved, especially at brand-name dealers. Many have a used-car inspection program that certifies the quality of the used cars on their lots. And most of the cars still smell pretty good.

Steer Clear of Car Loans

Purchasing a new car is not the only way to pay too much for a car. Purchasing a car with a loan is another way to ensure that you will pay more than you should.

Let's say you purchase that new car for $30,000 with a loan for the entire amount. The interest rate on the loan is 6 percent. The payments run for five years. If you don't pay the loan off early, you end up paying $4,800 in interest. That $30,000 car purchase turns into a $34,800 car purchase.

One of the more common financial challenges people face is having a loan that is greater than the value of the car. Given how quickly cars depreciate, it's easy to see how this happens.

Once again, assume you purchase a new car for $30,000. Once you drive off the lot, you suddenly owe $30,000 on a car worth $27,000. Right away, you are upside down (owing more than the value of the car) on the car. And this can continue while depreciation outpaces the amount you are able to pay down on the loan. Long-term loans, lasting five to seven years, are notorious for getting people upside down on their car.

You don't want to find yourself upside down on a car loan, especially if you need to get rid of the car. Many find themselves unable to make their car payments. So they decide to get rid of their car. But they find themselves unable to. Not surprisingly, people only purchase cars for what they are worth, not what covers the loan.

Trying to rid yourself of a car on which you are upside down can be messy.

So, what do you do? Here are a few suggestions:

1. **Know what you owe.** This will be your starting point. Figure out how much negative equity you have in the car. In our example, you owe $30,000 with $3,000 in negative equity.
2. **Don't trade in.** Trading in your car at a dealership is usually the worst financial move to make. The dealership will take your negative equity and place it on the new car you purchase. So you really aren't eliminating your negative equity. And you may find yourself even more upside down on your new car. Additionally, the new interest rate may be higher, causing you to pay more for that $3,000. Sometimes a cash-back offer can help balance out the negative equity, but be very, very careful before doing this.
3. **Pay down the loan with cash.** This is the best option. Pay down your car loan and sell the car. If you don't have the money

to do this, maybe you can find a few items in your house that you can sell to raise some quick cash.

4. **Refinance with a shorter term.** If you are struggling with the monthly payment or needing to sell your car immediately, this is probably not an option for you. A shorter term will result in a higher monthly payment, but you will pay down the loan (and get out of the negative equity position) more quickly.

5. **Take out a loan for the amount owed.** Admittedly, these are tough to get because they are unsecured. But check with your local bank or whoever holds your current car loan. Using our earlier example, use a $3,000 loan to get the car sold and pay off the loan. Of course, this means that you still owe $3,000. But you would rather have a $3,000 loan you can afford than a $30,000 loan you cannot afford.

Now, go get a really cheap car until you can afford something else. Buy what you can actually afford. That is the best decision you can make.

If you are considering a car purchase, buy used. Let someone else eat the several thousand dollars that come along with a new car. New cars are simply not worth the costs.

And avoid car loans. Your best option is to pay cash, even if this means you have to get a lesser car.

How to Destroy Debt

When it comes to getting out of debt, there is no easy button. It takes passion and persistence. It takes self-control and accountability. You must have the deep desire to get out of debt and the drive to keep going even when you feel like you want to quit.

Here's the good news—with passion and persistence you can get out of debt. You can get rid of that weighty burden that hangs over you and your spouse. You can get rid of that mess that hinders your ability to give generously and save wisely.

You may have heard of the Snowball Method. The Snowball Method is a widely used plan to get help people get rid of their debt. For some time, Dave Ramsey and others have championed the Snowball Method.

The method is easy to understand. Here is how it works—pay off your debts (not including your home mortgage) in order of lowest balance to highest balance. And that's it.

Imagine you have the following four debts:

- $5,000 car loan with a 6% interest rate
- $10,000 credit card balance with a 19% interest rate
- $27,000 student loan with a 5% interest rate
- $250 credit card balance with a 19% interest rate

To follow the Snowball Method, place these debts in order of lowest balance to highest balance. The order should look like this:

- $250 credit card balance with a 19% interest rate
- $5,000 car loan with a 6% interest rate
- $10,000 credit card balance with a 19% interest rate
- $27,000 student loan with a 5% interest rate

So your first debt to tackle is that $250 credit card balance. Taking out the first debt creates a sense of excitement and optimism about the ability to get debt-free. Like a snowball rolling down a hill, momentum is created, motivating you to take on the next smallest debt.

This is a plan that anyone can follow. All you need to do is lay out your debts on your coffee table, and identify which one you will target first. And then get started.

Of course, don't forget to pay whatever minimum payments are due on your other debts. To focus on one debt does not mean to completely ignore the rest.

Now Is the Time

Destroy your debt. Debt will cause both mental and financial stress. It will hurt your present and future. It will kill your ability to live the generous life God designed you to live.

If you are currently debt-free, congratulations! Decide to stay that way. If you and your spouse do have debt, whether little or much, use the Snowball Method to get rid of it.

Determine that you and your teammate are going to eliminate the burden of debt. Determine to no longer be a slave to the lender.

Your Marriage Challenge

Day 14 Marriage Challenge: *Get your debt snowball rolling.* Put all of your debts, except for your mortgage, in front of you. Order them from smallest balance to largest balance. This is the order in which you need to pay off your debt. Now go do it!

CHAPTER 9

You're Unemployed. Now What?

After breakfast the next morning, Chris and Claire took their coffee to the pool deck to sit down and look out onto the beach. There were a few people walking. One was running. And one family was already claiming their spot for the day.

"They're a pretty ambitious family," Claire joked, pointing at the family with her coffee mug.

Chris didn't say anything.

"Are you okay, Chris? You have been quiet all morning."

Again, Chris was silent. But then he pulled out his phone and read out loud an email from one of his coworkers.

Chris,

I just thought you would want to know that I was notified of my layoff yesterday. They are giving me severance pay, but they want me out of the office by the end of the week. I am sorry to tell you this on your honeymoon, but I will already be gone by the time you get back. I have enjoyed working alongside you. I am sure I will talk to you later.

Jerry

Chris slouched over.

"I'm sorry, Chris," said Claire. "But it doesn't mean you'll lose your job. You just don't know."

"Look, if Jerry is gone, I'll probably get the ax soon as well. The company is cutting pretty deep this time. There will be a lot of layoffs." Chris took a deep breath, "I need to get my résumé together."

Claire put her arm around Chris. "It will be okay."

Just then, Terry and Mary walked up from a morning stroll on the beach. They noticed Chris and Claire and made their way over to them.

"What's wrong? Did that family take your spot on the beach?" Terry said in an attempt to lighten the mood.

Chris briefly looked up at Terry and Mary and then looked back down. "I wish that were the problem. I just received an email from one of my coworkers who was laid off. More than likely, my job will be cut shortly."

"Man, I'm sorry, Chris. I know what it feels like," said Terry.

Chris responded, "You own your own business. Did you fire yourself?"

Terry chuckled, "No, I didn't fire myself. I didn't always own the auto shop. Before the shop, I worked for an automobile parts manufacturer. I was a manager, but then the automobile industry started to decline. And my job went with it."

Chris looked up. It did make him feel a little better that this rich guy could relate. It gave him a slice of hope.

Mary then spoke, "Yes, it was scary. If we hadn't saved six months of living expenses, we would have been a lot more panicked than we were."

"Six months of living expenses? That's impressive," said Chris.

Mary replied, "Well, it didn't happen overnight. We saved for a while. We wanted to get anywhere between three and six months. But once we hit three months, we just decided to keep going."

Chris and Claire looked at each other. They had a lot of work to do in this area of their finances.

Terry spoke, "Look Chris, I think you'll be fine, even if you get laid off. There will be another job opportunity out there for you. If you want to move to Chicago, you can always work for the auto shop! Or, you could stay here and work at the resort!"

Chris smiled. "I think I'm more of a Miami guy than a Chicago guy."

Mary grinned and replied, "You've obviously never tried our pizzas."

"Not yet," Chris replied.

"Chris," Terry said, "you are going to be fine." Terry patted Chris on the back. "We're going back in. See you guys later."

"Bye!" said Claire.

Chris looked out onto the beach again. "That family did get a really good spot, didn't they?"

"The best spot ever," Claire said with a smile.

As they continue to look at the beach, Chris pulled out his phone and typed:

5. Save money for job loss.

———————

Money Milestone 5: Save Three to Six Months of Living Expenses

Few could have anticipated the fallout that occurred in 2008. The market had tanked, and companies were feeling the financial pinch. Massive layoffs ensued.

In 2008, 2.6 million jobs were lost. In just the month of December, 524,000 of those jobs were lost. Merry Christmas. By the year's end, the unemployment rate had hit 7.2 percent.[1]

I worked for a church during that period and watched church member after church member lose their job. I have never received more résumés than I did in 2008 and 2009. They were desperately seeking work, any work. Most were willing to take a job that was well below their experience and skill set. They just needed some income.

Like millions of people that year, they never thought they would find themselves in this position—talented, well educated, experienced, and jobless.

This Is a Job-Loss Emergency

The second Milestone was to set aside $1,500 for a minor emergency. Hopefully, this minor emergency fund would be enough to cover a car repair or replace a busted hot water heater.

If only these types of emergencies were all with which we needed to concern ourselves.

But you know there are greater challenges out there. Like many in 2008, you may have already faced a much greater financial emergency than needing a new car tire.

If 2008 taught us anything, it taught us to be prepared. In fact, for many Millennials, 2008 shifted their view of employment and employers. Many Millennial employees don't view themselves as employed for life at their companies. They have more of a contract work mentality, putting their trust in themselves rather than a company. They are not committed to the company because they don't believe the company is committed to them. So they remain mentally nimble, ready to move companies if necessary.

Major emergencies, like losing a job, are rare. They occur on a much less regular basis than minor emergencies. But when they do hit, their punch can be devastating. Losing a job can take a significant emotional and financial toll. For some, losing a job means selling a house, finding a new school for the kids, and, of course, finding a new job. Losing a job is stressful and exhausting.

And if you aren't prepared, you can quickly find yourself with an empty bank account.

How Much?

Well, it depends.

A job-loss emergency fund should have enough in it to cover three to six months of living expenses.

But where do you fall in that range?

To determine what this number is for you, take a look at your monthly bills. Identify your essential bills. How much do you pay for housing (monthly payment, utilities, and insurance), food, health, and necessary transportation (including insurance)? Certainly, items like cable television and your children's sports are nice, but I would not classify them as essential. Identify what is essential. Of course, you can always include more bills if you desire. But, at least include what is absolutely necessary.

Here is the "it depends" part. Whether you save three, four, five, or six months worth of living expenses depends on your financial responsibility for others and how many wage earners you have in the house. A single person can be more agile if they lose a job. So for a single person, my recommendation leans toward the three-month end of the spectrum.

But you aren't single. If you are financially responsible for your spouse, and maybe children, I lean more toward the six-month end of the spectrum. If both you and your spouse work, you may be able to reduce this amount slightly.

And be sure to get your teammate's thoughts on it. An emergency account can be surprisingly personal. My wife tends to like more in our emergency fund than I do. For her, it is more about a way to take care of our children. So we set aside whatever amount makes her feel comfortable. It is a simple sacrifice of preference on my part.

Remember, you and your teammate have different money personalities. Determining the amount you save for a job-loss emergency is just one of the many places where your personalities will show up.

Determine how much you need to save together. Because if a job is lost, both will feel the impact.

Where?

Your minor emergency fund should be in a place where you can access it quickly, probably a checking or savings account. For your job-loss emergency fund, the options broaden.

Certainly, a checking or savings account will work. But you probably will not need three to six months of living expenses immediately if you lose a job. Usually, you have some time to transfer from a place that might not be as easily accessed to a checking or savings account.

Why is this important to consider? You get little to no financial gain when keeping money in a checking or savings account. Which is a shame if you have three to six months of living expenses—usually a good chunk of money—set aside.

Some options you and your teammate may want to consider are a money market account, online bank savings account, or no-penalty certificate of deposit (CD). All of these options usually provide a higher interest rate than a traditional checking or savings account. You won't get ridiculously wealthy using any of them, but, of course, that is not the point of an emergency fund.

Leveraging Abundance

Proverbs 30:24–25 says, "Four things on earth are small, yet they are extremely wise: ants are not a strong people, yet they store up their food in the summer."

Ants leverage seasons of abundance for seasons of scarcity. We can learn a lot from this little bug.

Setting aside three to six months of living expenses is not a goal that's easily accomplished. Like all financial goals, it takes time and persistence. The good news for those pursuing this Milestone is that you have already rid yourself of all debt except a mortgage. So now you can shift the money you were spending on debt to your Job-Loss Emergency Fund.

Here are some thoughts on how to save money for this fund:

1. Monthly transfers. Set up automatic transfers from your checking account to wherever you decide to put your emergency fund. Make sure you don't forget to set aside money by making the transfers automatic. You can do this through your online bank account. Note: automatic transfers cannot go into a CD.

2. Occasional excess. There will be times when you find yourself with excess money. And I am not referring to large sums of money. There will be times when you will find yourself with an extra $20 or $50. Don't spend it. Instead, get it out of your hands and into your emergency fund. These small deposits will add up over time.

3. Tax returns. If you get a tax return, don't waste it. Many use their tax return as an excuse to splurge. Don't do that. Use your tax return in a way that you won't regret. Use the money to build up your emergency savings.

4. Bonuses. You work hard. And because of your excellent work, you receive a bonus. This probably means that you won't lose your job because of poor performance, but you can still lose your job for other reasons. Put work bonuses toward your emergency fund in case your company has to lay off even good employees.

You can set aside enough for your Job-Loss Emergency Fund. Leverage seasons of abundance. Be persistent and you can have three to six months of living expenses saved.

Protect those who rely on you. And protect your ability to live with open hands.

Now, let's get saving.

Your Marriage Challenges

Day 15 Marriage Challenge: *Learn from ants.* Read Proverbs 6:6–8 together. Discuss the verses. What do they mean for you and your finances?

Day 16 Marriage Challenge: *Talk about losing your job.* Sounds fun, right? Use these money and marriage conversation starters:

1. Who has been your favorite employer? Why?

2. What are our financial essentials?

3. Regarding the amount in our job-loss emergency fund, do you think we should lean more toward three months or six months?

CHAPTER 10

The Retirement You Always Wanted

Later that day, Chris and Claire found themselves trying to forget about the layoff by relaxing at the beach. They sat in a couple of beach chairs under a large umbrella. Chris was listening to music on his phone while Claire read a book she had bought at the resort's small shop.

Chris watched as people journeyed along the shore, some picking up shells, some splashing in the water as it rolled up onto the beach. A couple of young boys ran across the scene, chasing a few seagulls.

Not too far behind the seagull-chasing kids, an elderly couple walked by. They were talking and laughing and holding hands. Chris glanced over at Claire, who was apparently enjoying the book she bought. She had not looked up since she started it. He was grateful to be married to her.

The elderly couple made him think about the future of their marriage and money.

"Claire, do you remember the conversation I had with the resort staff member about retirement?"

"You mean the conversation where you told him they had jobs that didn't pay very much?"

"Uh, yes. That would be it. Do you think we'll have enough for retirement? I mean, do you think we'll be like that elderly couple, able to spend some time away together, or do you think we'll still be working just to survive?"

Claire thought for a few seconds. "Well, I hope we will have enough for some flexibility in our schedule."

"Me too. But the word *hope* scares me. My parents hoped that everything would turn out fine in the future. But they never did anything about it, other than hope. And now, all that hope and no action has led them to a pretty bleak financial picture. Growing up, I learned that hoping doesn't put money in your account. Action does."

Claire nodded her head. "Okay. What are you getting at?"

"I'm going to take advantage of our company's match, but I don't think it will be enough."

Claire responded, "So you want to put more money into retirement?"

"I do. After we pay off our debt. You getting laid off is a good reminder to not only be prepared for not working now but also for not working later. One day, as smart and good-looking as I'm sure I'll be in my sixties and seventies, it may be tough for me to get or keep a job. And if we don't have enough saved for retirement, we'll be working jobs we don't like."

Claire smiled. "Or, we could be like Mr. Gunther, working out of love and not obligation."

Chris sighed. "Well, I would be happy working here for the rest of my life too. Look at the place. But, more than likely, we aren't going to work at a luxury resort in Miami."

"You never know," Claire responded.

"I want our retirement to be focused on mission, not money. I want our retirement to be focused on helping others in need and leaving a God-honoring legacy behind."

"Mr. Gunther helps people in need," said Claire playfully.

Chris smiled back at her.

Just then, three seagulls rushed by them, one flying right over Chris's and Claire's lap. Chris and Claire both yelled and tried to jump out of the way. But instead, both tripped over their chairs and fell into the sand.

Chris and Claire looked at each other, wondering what just happened. But then two young boys ran up.

"We're sorry. We didn't mean to chase them to you," said one of the boys. They were the ones Chris saw earlier.

Still in the sand, Chris replied, "No worries. What are your names?"

"Nathaniel and Joshua," the boys replied.

"Nice to meet you, Nathaniel and Joshua. I think your birds went that way." He pointed toward the seagulls, still distancing themselves from the boys.

And with that the boys ran off, kicking up some sand onto Chris and Claire.

The couple looked at each other, sitting on the beach, covered in sand. Both erupted into laughter.

As Chris dusted sand off of him, he said to Claire, "Remind me to put this in my notes:

6. Save more for retirement.

"Will do," Claire said, still chuckling at what had just happened. "Do you sense that?"

"What?" questioned Chris.

"Oneness," Claire said with a smile.

"All I sense is a bunch of sand in my shorts right now," responded Chris as he took off toward the water.

———

Milestone 6: Put 15 Percent of Your Gross Income into Retirement

A beach. A hammock. A golf course. A fishing pole.

What images go through your mind when you dream about retirement?

Many consider rest and relaxation to be the primary activity of retirement. Or you might say that retirement is about the absence of activity.

But is this what God wants out of our post-paycheck years? Or does he want something different? Something better?

The golf course is good. So is the beach. And there are times to enjoy those things.

But do you really want the focal point for your last tour of duty to be you? Or when your life comes to an end, do you want to look back on the last quarter of your life and remember the times when you lived something greater, something more adventurous, something bigger than yourself?

Sure, you may retire from a job. But you never retire from God's mission. The Christian's retirement should look different, not defined by today's cultural norms.

Because we are driven by something different, retirement becomes something different.

First, retirement becomes about them. The Great Commission does not stop when your retirement starts. It is a command Jesus gave us that we are to obey from the moment we become Christians to our death. There is no exclusion for retirement years. So retirement is just like every other year in a Christian's life—less about you and more about those who must hear the gospel.

Second, retirement becomes about mission, not lounging. While certainly there is a time to relax and enjoy the fruit of your labor, retirement is not a time for Christians to let off the gas. So if you need to take a rest in a hammock, go for it. But do not neglect the mission of which you get to be a part. No golf score can compete with the thrill you will get when your Father says those words, "Well done, good and faithful servant."

Third, retirement becomes about open hands, not tight grips. Some retirees find themselves with fewer bills and more resources. This is great news. It means you have planned well. But the retirement years are not yours to keep resources to yourself. Use your financial health to benefit others. Keep your hands open, use your resources for kingdom advancement.

Fourth, retirement becomes about getting involved, not playing hooky. You have knowledge, experience, and time that churches and people need. You possibly have more to bring to the table now than at any other point in your life. Get involved in your local church. Retirement is the perfect time to serve at your greatest level yet.

Finally, retirement becomes about breaking the retirement mold, not staying in the ordinary. The Christian's retirement is anything but typical. It is another chapter in your life's adventure as a believer in Christ. God designed you for mission, for openhandedness, and for involvement. The Bible does not tell us to spend the latter years of our lives in constant pursuit of relaxation. It tells us to go. It tells us to finish the race. It is a retirement plan that is anything but ordinary.

So prepare to retire in a way that fills your soul. Prepare well so that you can experience a generous retirement.

How Much Do You Need to Retire?

A few chapters back, we discussed compounding, employer-sponsored plans like a 401(k), 403(b), and 457(b), and why you need to take advantage of your employer match. For many, this is the starting point for retirement planning.

But will it be enough? Probably not.

Most financial professionals these days recommend setting aside about 15 percent of your gross income. I know—this seems like a lot. But you need a good chunk of money for retirement.

Let's simplify retirement income for a second. Assume that you desire to have $40,000, in addition to Social Security, each year for retirement. You think that amount is sufficient to cover your retirement plans. If you want your retirement investments to produce $40,000 without reducing the core of your funds, you probably need about $1,000,000 in your retirement account.

The exact amount you will need for retirement depends on your lifestyle expectation, age, and amount already saved. However, if you are young and begin putting 15 percent of your gross income into retirement, you are off to a great start.

Personal Plans

Companies and organizations can offer what's called employer-sponsored plans. But these are not your only retirement savings option. The government has made available what are called personal plans. Personal plans are not attached to an employer. And unlike employer-sponsored plans that limit investment options, personal plans allow you to choose almost any investment you like.

IRA stands for Individual Retirement Arrangement. There are two main types of IRAs—Traditional IRAs and Roth IRAs. Let's take a look at them.

Traditional IRA

Like a Traditional 401(k), contributions to a Traditional IRA can be tax deductible. You do still pay taxes, just later. Traditional IRAs are tax-deferred. So while the investment grows tax-free, you pay taxes when you take the money out of the Traditional IRA. The amount you take out is treated as regular income.

The government does not place any income limitations on these accounts, so anyone can contribute to them. But there are some contribution limits. As of 2017, you can contribute a maximum of $5,500. Those over fifty years old can contribute an additional $1,000 ($6,500).

There is a penalty for early withdrawal. If you withdraw before you turn 59½, there is a 10 percent penalty in addition to regular income taxes.

Roth IRA

Unlike a Traditional IRA, contributions to a Roth IRA are not tax deductible. The money you contribute to a Roth IRA has already been taxed. However, you do not pay any income taxes on the amount you take out of the Roth IRA. This can be a substantial future benefit.

Not everyone can contribute to Roth IRAs. Income limitations are placed on them. For single tax filers in 2017, the ability to contribute completely phases out once you pass $133,000 in annual income. For those filing jointly, the ability to contribute is not available to those couples earning $196,000 or more.

The maximum contribution is the same as the Traditional IRA. The early withdrawal penalty is the same as well (10 percent). But, unlike the Traditional IRA, you do not have to pay income taxes.

So Which One Is for Me?

Remember, the goal is 15 percent of your gross income toward retirement savings.

I am going to go ahead and assume that you are taking full advantage of your employer match, if that opportunity is there for you. Therefore, part of your 15 percent is already accounted for.

So now you are determining where to put the rest of that 15 percent.

If this is the case, or if a match is not available to you, I recommend getting a Roth IRA. The primary reason is for the tax-free withdrawals. I have no clue what taxes will look like in the future, and neither do you. Tax-free withdrawals create a level of certainty surrounding an uncertain topic. With Roth IRAs you do not have to worry about future tax rates.

So, what is the downside of setting up your own Roth IRA? You must remain disciplined. Employers typically route after-tax dollars to their employees' personal retirement accounts. More than likely, you need to set up the transfer from your checking account. Just don't fall into the temptation to use it for something else before the transfer day hits.

What about a Roth 401(k) or Roth 403(b)? This is also a good option. Since your employer holds the account, it may be the better option for those who struggle with financial discipline. With these accounts, your employer will take after-tax income and put it in the account. So the money never shows up in your checking account, eliminating the temptation to spend it. However, your investment options will be limited.

Try to keep retirement saving as simple as possible. Once you start to feel overwhelmed, giving up becomes significantly easier. It would be much better to have all 15 percent going into your Traditional 401(k) than not going anywhere at all. And honestly, if you have 15 percent going into any retirement account, you are way ahead of most.

When it comes to chasing financial health, simplicity leads to success. So keep it simple to keep it going.

When Fear Costs You a Generous Retirement

I hated the conversation.

Barry was an older pastor, ready for retirement. He came to meet with me because he had heard that I might be able to give him some advice. I could, but I knew my advice wouldn't be what he desired to hear.

As I looked over his retirement savings, I saw the picture of someone who had started saving for retirement late in his adult years. He had tried to catch up, but the battle was entirely uphill. Regardless, he plowed money into his investments.

I look at the performance chart, which revealed how his investments faired. For many years, the investments continued to go up. Year after year they performed well. And for a while, it looked like he would be able to scrape into retirement.

But then the market tanked.

And so did his investments. Down went the line on his performance chart.

He wanted to see what adjustments he could make to get out of this mess. But there were no adjustments to be made. I gave the only advice I could.

"Keep working."

Had he started saving for retirement earlier, he could have weathered this storm. There would have been enough in his plan.

But he started planning late, and now it required him to work longer. His heart was saddened, and so was mine.

I wish his story were abnormal. But you and I know that it is not. The Bible tells us the importance of preparing for the future:

> Idle hands make one poor, but diligent hands bring riches.
> The son who gathers during summer is prudent; the son
> who sleeps during harvest is disgraceful. (Prov. 10:4–5)

Many are starting too late and saving too little. Some are acting as if everything will somehow work itself out when retirement hits. But the man or woman who has reached retirement age without saving enough to make retirement a reality will tell you otherwise.

Hope does not get you to retirement. Habit does.

One of the reasons people postpone saving for retirement is fear. And this fear can look different from person to person.

Here are five fears that may be costing you, and many others, your retirement:

1. Fear of complexity. You think investing is for those with finance degrees. And while I do have one of those, I can tell you that there are many men and women who are successfully setting aside money in mutual and index funds every month who do not have a financial background. Investing does not have to be overly complex. Just a basic understanding can go a long way toward achieving your retirement goals.

2. Fear of losing money. Markets go up, and markets go down. There will be times of great financial gains and times of financial losses. Don't fear losing money—expect it. But also expect a future gain. If you diversify your investments well, you should expect an overall healthy, long-term growth of your retirement funds.

3. Fear of wrong timing. I've seen this fear creep up in several people since 2008. They wonder if they should wait to invest until the market conditions are perfect. Here's the reality—neither you nor I know when that may be. Those who wait for optimal conditions tend to miss out on gains in their retirement account. Timing the market is difficult. The best practice is to habitually invest every month, whether the market is up or down.

4. Fear of the wrong investment. I understand the reason for this fear. The last thing you want to do is invest in a mutual fund that has subpar performance. First of all, it is wise to discuss your investment selections with a financial advisor. Second, you can do your own research as well. As you look at investments, consider their long-term performance and fee structure. There are plenty of sites like Morningstar.com to help you with it.

5. Fear of missing out. Many choose not to invest simply because they want to spend the money on something now. They don't want to miss out on a certain lifestyle that limits their ability to save. Unfortunately, this fear will catch up to them, and their fear will become reality. Eventually, they will no longer be able to support their lifestyle, and they really will miss out, especially when retirement hits.

Remember the Formula

A little bit of money plus a lot of time can equal a lot of money. Don't miss out on prime years for living generously. Prepare for retirement. Set aside money today for your future, kingdom-advancing retirement years. And remember, if you are unsure where to start, consider a target fund.

Your Marriage Challenges

Day 17 Marriage Challenge: Figure out how much you need to retire. There are plenty of retirement calculators online. Just do a quick search for one. If the result scares you, just remember *a little bit of money + a lot of time = a lot of money.*

Day 18 Marriage Challenge: *Have another retirement conversation.* Use these marriage and money conversation starters:

1. If you could pick someone's retirement to emulate, who would it be? Why?

2. What percent are you currently putting toward retirement?

3. What type of retirement savings plan do you think works best for you?

CHAPTER 11

The Big Purchases

Terry and Mary invited Chris and Claire to dinner at their suite again. The newlywed couple wouldn't miss the opportunity. How often do you get to see a "room" like that?

Chris and Claire told them about the two young boys who had chased the seagulls right toward their spot on the beach. Everyone had a good laugh about it.

"Just remember," said Terry, "One day, you two will probably have kids of your own, and they'll do something similar."

"Oh, if they have half the personality Chris does," said Claire, "I can guarantee we'll have more than a handful of embarrassing moments. I'm pretty sure we'll be saying 'I'm sorry' on a regular basis."

"Hey!" said Chris. "I would take offense to that if it weren't true."

Everyone laughed.

Just then, Claire's phone buzzed. It was notifying her of a new email. She took a quick look at it and rolled her eyes.

Claire said, "Speaking of kids, we better figure out a way to pay for our future kids' college so they don't have a bunch of student loan debt like me. I just got a notice that my bill was due."

"You need to get rid of that phone. All it does is give you bad news," commented Chris.

The couples heard a brief knock on the door and then the suite's door opened.

"Can we come in? We have your dinner ready," said an unfamiliar voice.

"Of course," said Mary.

The couples waited for Mr. Gunther to walk through the door, but he never did.

"Is Mr. Gunther off this evening?" questioned Mary.

One of the staff members replied, "Unfortunately, Mr. Gunther was not feeling well today. He went home to get some rest."

"Oh no," said Terry with concern. "Is everything okay?"

"The staff member answered, "We really hope so. It does take a lot to keep Mr. Gunther from the resort though. Keep him in your prayers."

The staff members set up dinner and left.

"I hope Mr. Gunther is okay," said Claire.

"Me too," said Chris.

The couples made their way to the balcony. Just like last time, Chris and Claire found themselves impressed. The experience was absolutely incredible.

"I think we've fallen in love with this resort," said Chris.

"It is a pretty special place, isn't it?" Mary responded.

"I'm sorry to hear about your student loan, Claire," Terry said. "Debt stinks. We hate it because it reduces our ability to be generous with our money. Unfortunately, student loan debt is crushing young adults now."

"Yes, it makes me want to ensure that our future kids won't have this type of debt," said Claire.

Mary spoke, "We started setting aside money for our children's college early too. I can't tell you how much that helped us and them.

They still had to work some during college, but they were able to graduate debt-free."

Terry interjected, "We also helped them choose affordable schools."

"Well, I'm jealous," replied Claire.

Terry responded, "Look, focus on knocking out your debt and saving for retirement. And, if you're able, set aside some money for future college expenses. But please focus on taking care of your own finances before you take care of their finances. Or else, they'll end up paying for you in the future."

Chris wondered if, one day, he would have to take care of his debt-ridden parent because of their money decisions. Terry was right. Saving for their kids' college was nice, but it was not the most important money decision they could make.

Even still, Chris took out his phone and made a note:

7. Save for college.

Milestone 7: Save for College or Pay Off Your Mortgage

Once you make it to Milestone 7, you have accomplished something significant. Your debt is paid off, you have a job-loss emergency fund, and you are putting 15 percent of your gross income into a retirement savings plan.

Now you have the option of either paying off your mortgage or saving for your children's college. If you have children, my recommendation leans more toward college savings.

If you are newly married, let's focus on what makes paying off your mortgage or working to ensure that your child has little to no student loan debt more attainable.

Smart purchase decisions.

Throughout your marriage, you will have the opportunity to make some big purchases. These purchases will often be accompanied by several zeros, entering into the tens of thousands (and sometimes, hundreds of thousands) of dollars.

Excitement will surround these purchases because of the way they affect your life. And while this excitement can be good, the sense of euphoria can also lead you to make unwise money decisions.

Your ability to pay off these big purchases begins before you actually make the purchases. If you start considering how to pay off your big purchases after you have signed on the dotted line, you are late to the game. Using future-focused, wise decision-making can significantly amp up your ability to pay off big purchases.

In this chapter, we are going to consider three big purchases that couples make. Two you can pay off. One just costs you.

Big Purchase 1: Where You Live (Your City)

Imagine you just received a job offer that included a $65,000 salary. Should you celebrate?

It depends.

Certainly, you would always rather have a job offer than a decline. But the extent to which you get excited about the job offer should, in part, reflect where the job is located.

Here's what I mean—a $65,000 salary is different in San Francisco, California, from a $65,000 salary Birmingham, Alabama. The numbers are the same, but what you can do with the money is dramatically different.

You have probably heard the term *cost of living*. Cost of living is how much money is required in a particular area to meet your everyday needs, including health care, housing, food, and taxes. The differences among cities can be fairly dramatic.

Housing in San Francisco is six times the national average. In Birmingham housing is one-third of the national average. In San Francisco, food is 20 percent higher than the national average. Birmingham's food cost is slightly below the national average. When placed side by side, Birmingham is 73 percent cheaper than San Francisco.[1]

Of course, most don't consider the financial implications of living in a particular place. We may desire to live in certain cities or towns for a variety of reasons, but cost rarely makes the list.

Cost of living is an often-overlooked factor that can have a huge impact on your ability to give generously, save wisely, and live appropriately. Most don't realize that your decision to move to a particular city or town is a purchase decision. You are agreeing to purchase everyday needs at either a premium or a discount. If you move to San Francisco, you are agreeing to housing costs that are well above the national average.

We live in a very transient world. People are moving to and from different cities on a regular basis. In most major cities, you meet very few people who are native to the area, having spent their entire lives in that one location. We move, sometimes out of necessity, sometimes out of desire—desire for a new experience.

"Where do you want to live?" is a common question asked by married couples. When my wife and I got married, we asked that question. I remember looking at a map and considering the possibilities. You probably have done something similar.

As you create your list of places to live, let me encourage you to consider cost of living and its consequences for your present and future financial well-being.

The following questions are worth asking:

Will my salary be adjusted for cost of living? Remember, a $65,000 salary goes a lot further in Birmingham than San Francisco.

Will we be able to afford the experience we want in that city? Many dream of an experience they can't really afford. Sometimes a city is a better vacation destination than a home.

Will we ever be able to purchase a home? For some couples, home ownership is a big deal. Some places make this more of a reality than others.

Will we be able to live generously, or will we be living pay-check to paycheck? When the cost of living is high, days are often marked by financial stress rather than enjoyment.

What are the taxes? Alabama and California have different sales and income taxes. Do you know what they are?

Will we be able to save? Will we be able to set aside 15 percent for our retirement years? Or will we look back on these years with financial regret?

Where you choose to live is really one big purchase decision. Before you decide to move, put together a quick budget that assumes the area's cost of living. Make sure you can afford your hometown.

Big Purchase 2: Where You Live (Your House)

There are many reasons couples desire to buy a house. For some, it symbolizes adulthood, that they've finally grown up. For others, it represents stability—homeownership announces that they are putting down roots. And for others, it is an investment, hoping that the home will increase in value over time.

All of these are good reasons for buying a home.

But if we stop here, we are missing one of the most important reasons.

Unfortunately, it is a reason that is often missed. So here it is—*homeownership is a long-term strategy to free up future cash flow.*

I know. This reason doesn't give you the feels like the other reasons. It seems so, well, calculated.

Because it is.

Today, many treat mortgage payments as just another part of life, like a water or electric bill. They have always had a mortgage and assume they always will. It is a depressing, costly, and self-fulfilling mind-set. Because mortgage loans are often stretched out to thirty years, we lose sight of one of the most important benefits to owning a home—the prospect of not having a house payment.

Not too long ago, people bought homes with the intention of actually paying them off quickly. They did not plan on making a mortgage payment for every month of their life, from early adulthood to late retirement.

That is no longer the case for most Americans. But it should be the case for you. You can be the couple in the neighborhood that doesn't use your home equity for nonemergency purchases. You could be the couple that, instead of upgrading your home when you get a raise, stays put, and uses the extra cash to pay down your mortgage. You could be the couple that sees homeownership as a long-term strategy to free up future cash flow. And if our aim is to live generously, freeing up future cash flow is incredibly helpful.

Consider this. What would your current financial picture look like without a house payment? What would your generosity look like? What would your stress look like?

Or, think about this—what would your future retirement look like without a house payment? A person's house payment is usually their largest single monthly bill. When you retire, your income will likely go down. But your house payment will not. So your house payment will take up an even larger portion of your income.

When you do retire, I bet you will want to use that money for something other than a mortgage payment.

Are You Ready to Buy a Home?

I don't think everyone should buy a home. In fact, there are times when renting is the wiser choice. You should only purchase a home when it makes financial sense.

To help you determine whether or not you should buy a home, let me ask you three questions:

1. Do you plan on living there for at least five years? Financial gains are easily erased if you sell your home before the five-year mark. First, you have several up-front fees that are associated with buying a home. Second, your mortgage payments are going to be interest heavy for a while, meaning the majority of your payments will go toward interest.

So the first few years of homeownership really don't do much for you financially. In fact, they can end up costing you. If you think you will move within five years, you may want to consider renting.

2. Will your mortgage payment be less than 30 percent of your after-tax pay? I can't tell you how many couples I have heard use the term *house poor* while referring to their finances. Being "house poor" means most of your money goes to paying your mortgage. Only after the purchase did they realize that they bought a home that did not fit their budget. It can be a frustrating scenario.

Give your budget some flexibility. Make sure your mortgage payment is less than 30 percent of your after-tax pay. For example, if your after-tax pay is $5,000, try not to take on a mortgage that is greater than $1,500 ($5,000 x .30).

3. Do you have at least 20 percent for a down payment? You can get a mortgage without having to place a 20 percent down payment on the house. But I generally don't recommend it.

If you aren't able to put down 20 percent of the home's purchase price, you are often hit with private mortgage insurance (PMI). Since you didn't put down 20 percent, you are considered a higher risk for the bank. In order to protect themselves, they make you pay for PMI every month along with your mortgage payment. Yes, PMI is to protect them from you.

Think about that for a second. It should cause you to pause before signing any loan documents.

PMI ranges from .3 percent to 1.5 percent of your original loan balance and usually continues until you have paid down 20 percent of the home's value. FHA loans, a type of loan insured by the Federal Housing Administration, also have mortgage insurance with different regulations. If you are considering an FHA loan, be sure to ask about how mortgage insurance works for the loan.

If you don't have 20 percent of the home purchase saved, you may want to wait. Not only will this help you avoid PMI, it will help you get financially prepared for homeownership.

Do you plan on living there for five years? Will your mortgage be less than 30 percent of your after-tax pay? And do you have at least 20 percent for a down payment? When you are able to answer yes to these three questions, you are probably ready for homeownership.

Of course, don't forget to consider all the other costs associated with homeownership. You can't call the landlord to fix your washer machine. You are the landlord.

Big Purchase 3: Where Your Kids Will Learn

The Millennial generation learned its lesson about college—it can be expensive. Many college graduates walked across a stage, were handed a diploma, and then entered into the world of debt repayment. So far, the Millennial generation has done a better job than past generations saving for their children's college, probably because they feel like they have to.

If you have children, saving for their college can be a huge blessing to them. One of my favorite ways to do this is through a 529 Plan. They are called 529 Plans because they are found in section 529 of the U.S. tax code. Genius. These plans are offered by individual states. And you can choose any of them. In fact, you can choose to have multiple states' plans simultaneously. So if you live in North Carolina, you can choose to have Alaska, New York, and Utah plans if you desire.

These 529 Plans are pretty easy to set up. Let's say you have collegiate hope for your son, Benny. Each plan can only have one beneficiary, so if Benny has a sibling, another account is needed.

When you contribute to the plan, funds go into the plan's investments. So, yes, risk is involved. Some states have multiple investment options from which you can choose. These funds' earnings grow tax-free. Once Benny goes to college, you can withdraw funds, tax-free, for qualified expenses. Qualified expenses include tuition, fees, books, supplies, and school-required equipment.

Your total contribution limits are really high. According to the IRS, contributions cannot exceed what you expect to pay for college. States can further define what this means. Limits can vary by state, but those limits get can as high as $500,000.

And you can change beneficiaries. If Benny graduates college with some funds still left in his 529 plan, you can change the beneficiary to your daughter Susie. There are some limitations for beneficiary change, but for most, 529s provide more than enough flexibility.

So, which 529 Plan do you choose?

With each state offering at least one option, how do you know which plan is right for you and Benny?

Here are three simple items to consider:

1. Ratings. How does the plan rank against other plans? Morningstar and savingforcollege.com are great resources when considering the comparative ranking of 529 Plans.

2. Returns. Historically, how have these plans performed? For these returns, be sure to look beyond just the most recent year. Consider five- and ten-year performances.

3. Rewards. Some states offer tax benefits for their residents who invest in their state's 529 Plan. If you are not a resident of that state, you are not able to receive those benefits. Determine whether or not you can receive any additional benefits for investing in your home state's plan. And determine whether or not these benefits are significant enough for you to not invest in another state's better performing plan.

The College Purchase Decision

Hopefully by the time your kids start receiving college acceptance letters in the mail, you have set aside a good amount of money in a 529 Plan.

But your work is not done. Your child still has to choose a school.

Most parents are highly influential in the selection process. While I don't recommend making your child's college selection for them, I do recommend helping them see the bigger picture by providing wise counsel.

Here are a few suggestions:

Dismantle the "high tuition means better education myth." Paying more for college doesn't mean you get a better education. Certainly, there are academically excellent schools that are expensive, but there are also many academically excellent schools that are a fraction of the cost.

The idea that receiving a high quality education must be accompanied by costly bills is not true. Show your future high school graduate some colleges that balance a lower cost with good academics.

Focus on net cost. Your net cost is what you actually pay after including grants and scholarships. Receiving a $20,000 scholarship for a school that costs $40,000 is certainly something to celebrate. But you are still left paying $20,000. This is your net cost. Compare this net cost to a school that costs $13,000 but without any grants or scholarships. Sure, you would love a few scholarships, but the reality is the net cost is still $7,000 less than the more expensive school. Over four years, this amounts to a $28,000 difference.

Show them the math. Focus on net cost.

Encourage rigorous scholarship and financial-aid searching. Even if the school's cost seems reasonable, seek out financial aid (not including student loans), grants, and scholarships. There are many opportunities out there to apply for funding. Most college students completely ignore these opportunities because it does take time and effort.

Encourage your child to put in the work. It's worth it.

Worry more about your child's character and grit than the school's name on the diploma. You probably know many people who just never seem to live up to their potential. And you probably know those who always seem to surprise you with their success. The school's name on the diploma is not worthless, but it by no means guarantees success.

Worry more about the person your child is becoming than the school they will attend. This will allow your child to experience more postcollege successes than a school's name on a diploma.

If you are providing financial help, set an amount. Make sure they know that you are not a money tree. Let them know how much you will help and encourage them to stick to a budget.

College expenses don't disappear when you graduate. You know this. You may be living it right now. They can follow graduates well into adulthood. Help your children make a financially sound decision for their college. Give them wise counsel so they don't graduate with a load of debt and a load of buyer's remorse.

Saving for your children's college is a good thing to do. But it is not necessary. Don't prioritize college savings above your retirement savings. As parents, we often want to sacrifice our own wants for the wants of our children. However, placing their college savings over your retirement savings will do more harm than good.

Adult children bear the weight of parents who did not prepare well for retirement. When it comes to taking care of college expenses, you have options. But when you retire, you either have enough or you don't. There are no do-overs.

Be good to your children by placing your retirement over their college expenses.

Purchase Wisely

Throughout your marriage, you and your teammate will likely get to decide on a number of big purchases. There will probably be a few cities with a few houses, and maybe some colleges too.

Decide not to let a dream purchase turn into a nightmare.

Think beyond the purchase and to the future financial ramifications. Don't let these big purchases injure your ability to live out God's design for you and your money. Don't let the allure of bigger, better, more luxurious, and more prestigious hinder your ability to be a part of advancing God's kingdom. Because no city, home, or college will ever give you the contentment you can get from aligning your life with his will.

Your Marriage Challenges

Day 19 Marriage Challenge: *Pray with your spouse about spending wisely together.* If you have a big purchase coming up, include it as you talk to God. You can use the following prayer to get started:

> *Give us the ability to resist the temptation to pursue purchases that are beyond our means. Help us make wise purchase decisions for the sake of our financial health and the ability to live generously.*

Day 20 Marriage Challenge: *Have a conversation about big purchases.* Use these money and marriage conversation starters:

1. Where is the most cost-effective, enjoyable place we could live?

2. Do you think we are financially ready to purchase a house?

3. How does your college experience impact the advice you would give to our children about selecting a college?

CHAPTER 12

Impact Eternity Together

A couple days later, Chris and Claire were walking through the resort lobby when they saw Mr. Gunther at the front entrance.

"Mr. Gunther!" yelled Claire as they made their way toward him.

Mr. Gunther turned and smiled. As Chris and Claire got closer, they could tell that Mr. Gunther didn't look himself. His movements were less energetic. He seemed tired.

Claire spoke, "Mr. Gunther, how are you doing? The staff told us you were sick. We've missed seeing you the past few days. We were worried about you."

"Oh, you don't need to worry about me. I'll be fine. I'm sorry I missed seeing you at dinner in Terry and Mary's suite. I planned on being there, but I just didn't feel well and decided to go home and rest."

"No need to apologize at all," said Chris. "We're just glad you're back. Dinner was incredible, as always."

Mr. Gunther gave a weak smile, "I am glad you liked dinner. Have you enjoyed getting to know Terry and Mary?"

"Oh, they are a great couple," replied Chris. "We've learned a lot from them. They've helped me understand that financial health is simply a means to something much greater."

"Interesting. Go on," encouraged Mr. Gunther.

"Well, we want the way we use money to bring contentment and purpose. We experience contentment and purpose when we are generous, using our money for something bigger than ourselves. This is because we are aligning ourselves with God's design for us and our money. Generosity allows us to make an eternal difference with our money."

Mr. Gunther was clearly impressed. "That's wonderful, Chris."

Chris continued, "But Terry and Mary are not the only ones I've learned from. You reminded me about pursuing oneness in marriage. So imagine what can happen when a couple pursues oneness and generosity simultaneously."

"I like how you're thinking, Chris," Mr. Gunther responded.

"Man, I'm going to miss this place," said Chris. "I'm starting to think that you have the best job in world," he said with a big smile.

Mr. Gunther lightly chuckled. "That's because I do." He then looked at Claire and back at Chris. "You two remind me so much of me and Rose when we first got married. You guys are going to turn out just fine."

Just then, a man wearing a suit walked up to the entrance.

"Mr. Gunther, it is so good to see you." The man in the suit reached out and shook Mr. Gunther's hand.

"Likewise, old friend," Mr. Gunther replied.

Then, Mr. Gunther turned to Chris and Claire, smiled, and said, "Excuse me, but I have a meeting with this great man."

"Of course, Mr. Gunther," Claire responded.

Mr. Gunther smiled again and pointed at Chris and Claire. "Both of you, live generously."

And with that, Mr. Gunther and the man in the suit walked away.

Chris took out his phone and typed:

8. *Live generously.*

Milestone 8: Live Generously

I love Luke 8:1–3.

It says this:

> Afterward he was traveling from one town and village to
> another, preaching and telling the good news of the king-
> dom of God. The Twelve were with him, and also some
> women who had been healed of evil spirits and sicknesses:
> Mary, called Magdalene (seven demons had come out of
> her); Joanna the wife of Chuza, Herod's steward; Susanna;
> and many others who were supporting them from their
> possessions.

Right before these verses, Luke tells the story of Jesus, who was at
Simon the Pharisee's house. While they were eating, a woman, only
identified as a sinner, entered the room and stood at Jesus' feet and
began crying. The tears rolled from her eyes, to her cheek, to her chin,
and dripped onto Jesus' feet.

As if this were not shocking enough, the lady let down her hair—
which was considered shameful during that time—and wiped the tears
with her hair. She then kissed and perfumed his feet.

Simon could not believe that Jesus would allow himself to be
touched by this sinner. In his mind, he questioned Jesus' identity.

But Jesus knew his thoughts and responded to Simon by asking
him a question.

> "A creditor had two debtors. One owed five hundred dena-
> rii, and the other fifty. Since they could not pay it back, he
> graciously forgave them both. So, which of them will love
> him more?" (Luke 7:41–42)

Simon correctly chose the one who had been forgiven more.

Jesus pointed out that the woman's actions were the result of her understanding the extent of her forgiveness, unlike Simon, who considered himself in little need of forgiveness.

She had been forgiven much. Therefore, she loved much.

Fast-forward to the three women—Mary Magdalene, Joanna, and Susanna—in Luke 8, with the story of the "sinner" echoing in the background. These women had been healed of sickness and demon possession. By all indication, they realized, just like the woman in Luke 7, that they had been forgiven much. So they followed Jesus.

Here is what we learn from these women:

1. Those who are forgiven much, love much. Our love is to be first directed toward God and then to others (Matt. 22:37–39). These women understood the grace they had been given. So they set everything aside and followed Jesus. They loved God much.

But it didn't stop there. It couldn't stop there. Because when we love God, we love the things he loves. We prioritize the things he prioritizes. Which is everyone else.

So their love was directed toward others.

How do we know this? They were supporting *them* with their possessions. You see, when you love others, you put others first. And when you put others first, generosity is the outcome. This leads us to the second point.

2. Those who love much are generous with much. These ladies used what God had given them to support the mission of Jesus. Now why did Luke mention Joanna's husband, Chuza? Chuza managed Herod's household. This means they were probably fairly wealthy. More importantly, it shows that God is really the owner of everything, and he will use it all to carry out his plan. You see, this Herod is the same guy that participated in the beheading of John the Baptist and the crucifixion of Jesus.

God literally orchestrated a plan to use the resources that were under a man who was a part of Jesus' crucifixion to advance his kingdom. Herod's money was going to a family that used those funds to support Jesus. It not a question of whether God will use your resources to advance his kingdom. He will. He will use it all.

I love how J. D. Greear puts it: "God is going to win. The only thing you need to be concerned about is whether or not you will be invested in the process."[1]

Those who love much are generous with much. They are invested in the process.

3. Those who are generous with much impact eternity. These women did not have to wait until heaven to see the impact of their generosity. In Luke 24, we find some women arriving at Jesus' tomb with spices. But Jesus wasn't there. These women were first to see and hear that Jesus had risen from the dead.

And who is named as part of this group?

Mary Magdalene and Joanna.

They were the first to see the empty tomb—how's that for getting a return on your investment?

They were forgiven much, so they loved much. They loved much, so they were generous with much. They were generous with much, so they impacted eternity.

What about you?

Above and Beyond Giving

You may have noticed in The Takeoff (Milestone 1) I suggest your first 10 percent go toward the local church. The local church should be your first place of giving. But this is by no means where generosity stops.

Like the Macedonians in 2 Corinthians 8, those who live generously often find themselves desiring to do and give more. Often, this is the place of their greatest discontentment, as they never feel like they give enough.

So, what do you do when you reach that 10 percent mark?

Consider giving more to your local church. The local church is God's primary plan to advance his kingdom. The local church impacts individuals, communities, and the world. So consider increasing your giving to the church you attend.

Consider giving to another kingdom-advancing nonprofit organization. There are many good kingdom-minded organizations out there. And you may have a passion for a particular cause—feeding the hungry, orphan care, or medical ministries. Consider giving to an organization that shares your same passion.

Set aside some money for unexpected needs others face. People in your community are going to get hit with unforeseen emergencies. What if you had some money set aside specifically to meet those needs? How awesome would it be if God used you and your preparation to assist others with unexpected medical bills, car repairs, or just a lack of money to purchase basic needs? These are your "ready-to-give opportunities."

There is no right or wrong choice with this. Set a goal to give 10 percent to your local church. Then figure out what God would want from you next. What should your above-and-beyond giving look like? How can use your generosity to change lives and advance his kingdom?

Live Generously

God designed us not to be hoarders but conduits through which his generosity flows. When you and your teammate find yourself experiencing the fruit of sound financial decisions, you will be able to live more generously than you ever thought possible.

Suddenly, the financial shackles that held you down for so long are gone. You can react more quickly. You can respond to needs more readily. You can give more.

And you will experience contentment in this. You will be content, knowing that you are living for something beyond yourself. You will be content, knowing that you are invested in the advancement of God's kingdom.

This is the goal. This is the "why" behind the pursuit of financial health. Like the servants in the parable of the talents, we steward our resources well so that our Master's wealth increases. And so that we can hear those words—*Well done, good and faithful servant.*

Your Marriage Challenges

Day 21 Marriage Challenge: *Help your neighbor.* Identify a way that both of you can help one of your neighbors. Do they need babysitting? Do they need someone to mow their lawn? If you are not sure what they need, ask.

Day 22 Marriage Challenge: *Talk about living generously.* Use these marriage and money conversation starters:

1. What would life look like if we made it to Milestone 8?

2. How does understanding your forgiveness influence your generosity?

Decide to Destroy Marriage Dividers

Marriage and money issues are usually not about money. There is something deeper and more dangerous occurring. It just happens to reveal itself in your finances. Poor communication, selfishness, distrust, and unrealistic expectations often find their way into a marriage's finances. You must intentionally go after these marriage dividers.

Don't do it for your financial health.

Do it for your marriage.

CHAPTER 13

Marriage Divider 1—Poor Communication

The next morning, Claire decided to sleep in again, so Chris went to the resort restaurant to eat breakfast alone—or so he thought.

When he arrived, he saw Terry sitting at a table by himself, midway through a slice of bacon. Chris approached him and asked, "Do you mind if I join you?"

"No, not at all. Mary wanted to get some more sleep so I just decided to come down here by myself."

Chris smiled. "Same story here."

As Chris ordered his breakfast, he told Terry about his run-in with Mr. Gunther yesterday.

Terry expressed his concern about Mr. Gunther. "Man, I really hope he's alright. I'm not surprised he came back though, even if he didn't feel well. He really loves this place."

Terry looked at Chris. "You know, Mr. Gunther likes you and Claire a lot. I think you remind him of Rose and himself when they were newlyweds."

Some noise caused Terry and Chris to quickly turn their heads toward the front entrance. There was some commotion occurring with a few staff members. This was weird for the resort. They tried to ignore it.

"He mentioned that to us," replied Chris. "Hey, after listening to you and Mr. Gunther, I've put together a plan for my and Claire's money. We have a long way to go, but I'm pretty excited about it. What do you think?"

Chris pulled out his phone and showed Terry his steps.

1. *Start giving.*
2. *$1,500 minor emergency fund.*
3. *Get employer match.*
4. *Get rid of debt.*
5. *Save money for job loss.*
6. *Save more for retirement.*
7. *Save for college.*
8. *Live generously.*

"I love it," said Terry with a smile.

Terry questioned, "Hey, did Mr. Gunther ever tell you about the marriage dividers?"

"Marriage dividers?" Chris's response made it obvious that he had never heard of them.

"Yes. Marriage dividers. There are four of them. Mary and I struggled early in our marriage. There were a lot of fights. We thought our struggles were because of money. That's what we argued about the most. But then we met Mr. Gunther while on vacation down here. He told us that most of the time, when couples argue over money, it is usually not really about money. Money is the symptom, not the cause."

"I'm listening," said Chris as he took a sip of his coffee.

Terry continued, "After thinking about it for a while, we realized that Mr. Gunther was right. Money wasn't the reason for our fights. There were deeper issues at play."

Terry clearly had Chris's attention. "So, what are the marriage dividers?"

"As I said, there are four of them." Terry counted them off on his fingers. "Poor communication, selfishness, distrust, and unrealistic expectations."

"Wow. I can already see how a couple of those are hurting us. And I see how they are destructive to oneness."

"Exactly," said Terry. "They can hurt all of us. Remember when I told you that marriage worked like a team? A team will never succeed when poor communication, selfishness, distrust, or unrealistic expectations are present. And often these will show themselves in your finances."

Now there were more staff members gathering at the front entrance. Some appeared to be in distress. A few were hugging. Even Terry and Chris's server briskly walked over to the growing crowd.

"Something's wrong," said Terry. He got up and quickly walked over to the group of staff members. Chris followed.

Terry pulled the first staff member he could aside and asked him what had happened.

The staff member said through her tears, "Mr. Gunther died last night. He passed away in his sleep."

The staff member went back to console and be consoled. Terry and Chris stood there in shock for a few moments. Terry reached for his phone to wake up Mary.

"Mary, I have some bad news."

Communication Keys

Communication.

Whether you are a student, a businessperson, or a married person, you hear the word over and over.

Why? Because it is vital to any team's success *and* because we tend to struggle with it. Poor communication can create resentment, bitterness, and a lack of unity.

Poor communication is a marriage divider. And the lack of communication frequently reveals itself in a couple's finances.

But don't fret if you and your teammate find yourselves struggling with communication. There is hope. Good communication about your finances can be developed.

To guide you along on this journey, let me give you three keys for better marriage and money communication.

Key 1: Change Your Language

Words are powerful. You can probably remember words that cut you deeply ten or fifteen years ago. In fact, those words may still hurt. Negative words tend to linger longer than positive ones.

The words you choose to use communicate something to your teammate. And when it comes to money, your words will either communicate oneness or division.

When engaging in money conversations with your teammate, variations of the words *my* or *your* are two of the most harmful words to your oneness. Both words communicate singular ownership. "My" or "your" usually either shifts a burden disproportionately (usually with "your") or erodes a sense of valued input (usually with "my"). Neither is good.

Your credit card debt.

My checking account.

Your student loan.

My retirement savings.

You can sense the division.

Now enter one of the most unifying words in the English language—"our."

Our credit card debt.

Our checking account.

Our student loan.

Our retirement savings.

There is a real difference, one that moves beyond simple word choice. You can sense the oneness. Whereas the former phrases created a divide, suddenly, there is unity.

Individualism is replaced with cooperation.

For newlyweds, this can be a difficult shift. So be patient with yourself and your teammate in this area. Up until now, money was an individual issue. Your language reflected this reality. Now that money is a team issue, strive to use language that encourages cooperation.

We. Us. Our.

Let your word choice demonstrate that you are locking arms with them, and whatever the financial future brings, you will face it together.

Key 2: Budget

Budgets get a bad rap.

I am a University of Kentucky graduate, and, therefore, I get pretty passionate about their sports teams. You may have a team that you cheer for. Imagine if your team played a game without any plan. Entering the game, they had no clue what offense or defense to run. Apparently, they never really gave it much thought prior to the game. And when the coach was questioned about it later, he said, "I figured it would just work out in the end."

Or imagine that today is the first morning of your vacation. You are going to Oregon for the week. The family loads in the car, and you crank the engine. As you back the car out of the driveway, your teammate asks, "Do you know how to get there?" You respond, "Hadn't really thought about it. I assumed that if we just started driving, it would eventually work out."

We expect coaches to have a game-winning plan. And there is no way that you would waste your vacation traveling aimlessly. You would have a plan.

Well, that's what a budget is—a plan. A budget is your plan to accomplish your financial goals. It is your plan to pursue contentment and purpose in your finances.

A budget is also one of your most important tools to strengthen communication. Budgets force conversation. They get you and your teammate on the same page, moving forward in the same direction. My preference is a monthly budget. This fits most income and bill cycles.

If you haven't started a monthly budget yet, here are a few steps to get you going:

Step 1: Determine your monthly goals. Your first step in developing a monthly budget is to determine your financial goals, specifically your giving and saving goals. These goals will help define the shape of your budget.

If you haven't hit the 10 percent giving mark, I recommend it as goal. Likewise, if you haven't hit the 15 percent retirement goal, I recommend that goal as well.

Now, you may not be able to hit those goals this month, or even this year, but your monthly budget should reflect progress toward those goals.

For example, you may want to start The Takeoff plan for giving. This means including at least 1 percent giving. You may also consider dedicating a portion of your budget to retirement savings, a step toward hitting that 15 percent mark.

Make sure your budget allows you to take your next step in reaching your financial goals.

Step 2: Determine your monthly income. After identifying your financial goals, figure out how much you get paid on a monthly basis. Usually, this is a fairly easy step—simply look at your paycheck. If your pay varies, maybe because you are in sales, take the average of your past few months of income. Of course, if there happens to be a month where you received a much higher income than usual, exclude that month. Outliers can throw off your average.

More than likely, the income that shows up in your bank account is your net (after-tax) income. This is the amount you want to use for your monthly income.

However, if taxes are not taken out, which means you are probably self-employed, you will need to include your taxes in the next step.

Step 3: Determine your monthly expenditures. Next, go back and look at your past month's expenses. These expenses will serve as the starting point for step 3.

As you look through the expenses, consider whether or not you can lump any of them into a single category. This will simplify your budget. Complex budgets often result in abandoned budgets. Common categories include giving, saving, retirement, mortgage/rent, groceries, transportation, education, medical, and entertainment. Don't forget to include taxes if you used pretax income in step 2.

Step 4: Adjust your expenditures to fit your income (and your ability to save and give). Now add up all of your monthly expenditures. How do they compare to your monthly income?

For many, this reveals the reason for their financial struggles. They have more expenditures than income. Each month, they get a little further behind.

So, what do you do?

You adjust.

Look at your monthly expenditures and find places where you could cut back. For some, this may mean eating out less. For others, it may mean selling their current car and purchasing one that fits their budget. Even better, it means purchasing a car with cash and eliminating the ongoing monthly payment.

Don't forget to consider how you can include giving and saving in your budget. Giving and saving may be areas where increases are necessary. You may need to sacrifice a few good things for a much better thing.

Remember, your budget is a plan to help you reach your goals.

Step 5: Track your spending. After you have created your monthly budget, don't just set it aside and ignore it. Use it to make sure that your spending aligns with the plan.

There are many ways to track your spending. One of the most common, low-tech tracking methods is called the "envelope system." Each expense category receives its own envelope. For example, you probably would have an envelope titled "Groceries." In this envelope would be the amount you budgeted for the grocery category, in cash. As you make purchases, you use the money in the envelope. Once the money runs out, you don't make any more purchases.

The envelope system is designed to create financial discipline. And it has worked for many people.

If you prefer not having a bunch of cash in envelopes, there are several online budgeting resources. One is Mint.com. This digital platform connects your bank accounts to a budget you set up on the site. This is only one option—there are several other great online tools out there. The important thing is to find a way to keep up with your expenses.

Tracking your spending is vital to get out of a financial pit and on the track to financial health. Choose the tracking system that works best for you.

Step 6: Have a monthly check-in. Monthly check-ins is a great way not just to see if you are on track but to communicate with your teammate. Try to schedule some time each month to review your budget and make any necessary adjustments. Consider whether or not one-time expenses will hit in the next month. And don't forget to evaluate the progress you are making in reaching your goals.

Key 3: When in Doubt, Inform

What do you do when you need to make a budget-impacting purchase that you and your teammate have not discussed? This happens to my wife and me quite a bit. I've found myself needing to pay for a car repair that was more costly than I anticipated. Did I just not get my car repaired? Of course not. It needed to be done. But did I just go ahead and make the purchase and let my wife find out about it later? Nope.

I got her in the loop. I sent her a text, letting her know about the situation.

Financial surprises, especially on the expense side, rarely go over well with your teammate. Why? Because the expense is not *my* expense or *your* expense. It's *our* expense. The money you or your teammate spends impacts both of you.

You both have a limited amount of money, and when one uses part of that money, even for something necessary, it means that you both cannot spend that money elsewhere. The money is accounted for.

So to avoid surprises, inform your teammate. Maybe agree on a certain spending amount that requires both of you to be on board before making the purchase.

Now does this mean that every time you inform your teammate of a purchase, they will be on board with it? Hopefully not. Financial accountability is essential to moving forward.

There have been times when I got my teammate's input on a purchase I was considering, and her initial reaction wasn't positive—not because she was controlling but because she cared about the impact it would have on our finances. And this is good.

The wrong move would have been to go ahead and make the purchase. This only creates a divide in the marriage. The right move is to huddle up, listen, and figure out what the game plan needs to be moving forward.

Remember, oneness is more important than any purchase. Don't let a purchase cause your pursuit of oneness to stumble.

When in doubt, inform.

Destroy the Marriage Divider

Rich couples communicate well. They don't let poor communication create fissures in their marriage. They understand the power of words and try to use words that display unity instead of division. Rich couples try to limit financial surprises. They strive to keep their teammate in the loop.

Don't let poor communication divide your marriage and your finances.

Your Marriage Challenges

Day 23 Marriage Challenge: *Have a conversation about budgeting.* Use the following money and marriage conversation starters:

1. What has been your experience with budgets?

2. If generosity is our priority, how can a budget help us be more generous?

Day 24 Marriage Challenge: *Make a financial spending plan.* Some call this a budget. Use the six steps mentioned in this chapter.

CHAPTER 14

Marriage Divider 2—Selfishness

Claire and Mary made their way down to the resort entrance. They gave their husbands a hug.

"We were just talking to him yesterday," said Claire.

"I know," replied Chris.

They all watched as the crowd continued to grow. Now it was more than just staff members who were gathered. To the surprise of Chris and Claire, a couple of news stations came into the resort and started recording.

"Wow," said Chris. "Who would have thought that a greeter could have such an impact? It really is incredible."

Terry looked at Chris with an inquisitive expression on his face. "Did Mr. Gunther never tell you?"

"Tell us what?" asked Claire.

Terry replied, "Mr. Gunther was a great greeter. But he was an even better owner."

"Owner? Of what?" quickly questioned Chris.

"This," Mary said as she stretched her arms wide. "The resort. The Miami Palms Resort and Spa. He owned it."

Chris was shocked. "What? Are you serious?"

Terry provided some more details. "Yes. He and Mrs. Gunther became the owners a few years after they started working here. It was much smaller and not financially stable then. The original owner pretty much just gave it to them because he didn't want to deal with it anymore. Mr. Gunther grew the place by getting the staff to focus on one thing—guest experience. No one was above the resort's guests."

"Including Mr. Gunther," said Mary. "He was the standard-bearer here. He led by taking care of the guests and the staff."

"He and the resort are loved because of it," Terry said. "They're both legends in this area."

Chris's and Claire's heads were swirling.

Terry continued, "And I suppose he never told you about us."

"Do you own a resort too?" asked Chris.

Terry and Mary laughed. "No. We actually do own an auto shop. But we are by no means rich. Mr. Gunther calls us rich but not because we have a bunch of money. He calls us rich because of the contentment and purpose we found in our marriage and with our money."

Mary interjected, "For Mr. Gunther, that was rich."

"Well, you sure did have a nice suite for a couple without a ton of money," said Chris.

Terry smiled again. "That was from Mr. Gunther. He got to know us several years ago when we first vacationed here. I guess you could say that he just liked us. He helped us understand marriage and money better, and he was also incredibly generous to us."

"What an amazing guy," said Chris.

"He has left quite a legacy," responded Terry.

Mary spoke, "If we hadn't met Mr. Gunther early in our marriage, who knows where we would be?"

Terry replied, "Probably still fighting about money."

Mary grinned back at Terry.

———

Mine

I didn't realize how me-centric I was until I got married.

Before marriage, I was my own primary concern. My money was *my* money. I could budget and spend according to my preferences. Purchase decisions were no big deal. There was no one else to consider. No prepurchase calls or texts to make. No conversations needed. I bought my first townhouse without concern for anyone else's preference or desire.

I just needed to worry about me.

But then I got married. And God used marriage to help me understand how self-focused I was. He is still using marriage (and now children) to teach me about sacrifice, selflessness, and humility.

Selfishness is incredibly dangerous to a marriage. Its aim points directly against oneness.

No one is immune to selfishness. Each one of us has an inclination to do our own thing, to go our own way. "We all went astray like sheep; we all have turned to our own way" (Isa. 53:6).

Me-centric mentalities tear at the very heart of marriage. This is true not only for a couple's money but also for all areas of marriage. Selfishness is often the underlying issue for money problems that result in divorce. The couple may point at money as the problem, but they are really pointing at selfishness.

When we hoard, we depart from God's design for our money. Selfishness makes you poor, keeping you from experiencing the riches that God has in store for you. Likewise, selfishness makes your marriage poor. It causes you to miss out on the rich relationship between husband and wife that you really desire—one that can only be obtained through sacrifice.

The problem with selfishness is that it can be hard to identify in your own life. Here are a few signs that may indicate a me-centric mentality is present in you:

1. **You don't compromise.** Conversations about money are very one-sided. You argue until you get your way. You consistently think your teammate's desires are either unreasonable or uninformed. And if you don't get your way, you make sure that your teammate feels your unhappiness.

2. **You blame.** When something goes wrong, your teammate becomes your target. You find yourself blaming your teammate for your frustration and disappointment. You struggle accepting responsibility for your own actions. Even more difficult is owning the blame when your teammate makes a mistake. You avoid the opportunity to make it *our* mistake.

3. **You take the "It's easier to ask for forgiveness than permission" approach.** You don't ask because you don't want an answer that runs against your desire. You don't want input from your teammate. And even when you know your teammate would not be in favor of a financial decision, you do it anyway.

4. **You hide purchases.** Not only do you avoid your teammate's input, but you try to make sure that you do not have to ask for forgiveness. You try to make sure that they never find the purchase. You have a secret account. You have a secret credit card. You use cash so they can't track where you are spending your money.

5. **You are impatient with money decisions.** You know what you want, so why wait? You hate conversations about money decisions with your teammate because they delay your getting what you want.

6. **You don't want help.** You pride yourself on being independent. You pride yourself on being self-sufficient. But this is not God's design for marriage. Independence and oneness don't mix well; in fact, they don't mix at all. Rich marriages are dependent marriages. Each teammate depends on the other. Each teammate needs the other.

Selfishness versus Selflessness

It's funny to watch my kids play with their building blocks. My oldest son's goal is usually to build something really cool, like a big tower or a castle. My youngest son has a completely different goal. His goal is to knock down and destroy whatever my oldest son builds. You could say my youngest son is the archenemy of my oldest son's building plans.

The archenemy of selfishness is selflessness. Their goals are dissimilar in every way. Selflessness tries to put others before self. Selfishness tries to put self before others. In marriage, selflessness attempts to build and protect what selfishness tries to knock down and destroy.

Selflessness flows out of humility. And no one exhibited humility in a more powerful and perfect way than Jesus. Though God, he humbled himself as a human and was crucified for our sins. So it shouldn't surprise us that the Bible tells to follow Jesus and pursue humility.

> Do nothing out of selfish ambition or conceit, but in humility consider others as more important than yourselves. (Phil. 2:3)

> At that time the disciples came to Jesus and asked, "So who is greatest in the kingdom of heaven?" He called a child and had him stand among them. "Truly I tell you," he said, "unless you turn and become like children, you will never enter the kingdom of heaven. Therefore, whoever humbles himself like this child—this one is the greatest in the kingdom of heaven." (Matt. 18:1–4)

How do you pursue humility? How do you chase after this thing to combat the marriage divider called selfishness?

Focus on the holiness of God. *Holy* means "sacred or set apart." He is set apart because he is perfect, without sin, and cannot be in the presence of sin. By focusing on the holiness of God, you can't help but consider your lack of perfection and that it is only by God's grace that you can be considered right before such a holy God.

Remember who God defines as the greatest. In God's kingdom, everything is flipped on its head. The first are last. The last are first. We serve a God who exalts the humble. When you chase after selfish desires, you move yourself further to the back of the line.

Consider your place in the universe. You are one of more than seven billion humans on earth. You live on a tiny rock that revolves around one of potentially 1,000,000,000,000,000,000,000,000 (that's a septillion) or so stars in the universe.[1] And you have a God that made them all with his voice. You are small. We all are.

Reflect on your need for God every day. God is the sustainer and meaning provider of life. Not only does he give us the air we must breathe, but he gives us the meaning for life. We are totally reliant on him for everything.

Use your words to build up. Put your teammate before yourself with your words. Use your words to encourage your teammate. Identify the good you see in them. And tell them about it.

Listen. Often we are quick to tell others how we feel. We want to share our opinion first. Those who are humble learn to listen before speaking. Listening to your teammate communicates that you appreciate and value their thoughts and opinions, that they are worth hearing.

Pray. Spend one-on-one time with the God of this vast universe. Talk to him. Ask him to reveal the selfishness in your heart. Ask him to align your heart with his heart, to put others—namely, your teammate—before yourself.

Destroy the Marriage Divider

Sometimes, when a couple says that money issues caused their divorce, it really wasn't about the money. It was because one, or maybe both, of them put themselves first.

When a discussion about money took place, there was very little compromise: "It was my way or the highway." Or, maybe, instead of seeking out their teammate's input, they simply did what they wanted. They may have even hidden purchases and accounts from their teammate.

The divorce was not about the money. The divorce was about a me-centric heart.

Selfishness is worth fighting. Go to war with selfishness by pursuing humility. Build up oneness through sacrifice, selflessness, and humility. Don't let selfishness knock down the building blocks of your marriage.

Through humility, be a guardian of your marriage.

Your Marriage Challenges

Day 25 Marriage Challenge: *Write Philippians 2:3 on an index card.* Take the card and stick it on your bathroom mirror. Let it serve as a reminder to put your spouse and others before yourself.

Day 26 Marriage Challenge: *Have a conversation about humility.* Use the following money and marriage conversation starters:

1. In what situations do you find yourself battling selfishness the most?

2. Why is pursuing humility so difficult?

CHAPTER 15

Marriage Divider 3—Distrust

Later that evening, Chris and Claire were back in their room. They were leaving the next morning and decided to go ahead and start packing.

"You know, this wasn't quite the honeymoon I expected," said Claire.

"No kidding," responded Chris. "It has been unexpected in just about every way."

Chris folded a few of his clothes and placed them in their suitcase. The room was quiet. Both had a lot to think about.

Chris broke the silence. "I think the reason why I got so upset about your debt was less about the debt and more about a lack of trust."

"What do you mean?" questioned Claire. She stopped folding her clothes.

"Well, I just thought that in marriage couples were supposed to be transparent with one another. And you made me think that you were hiding something from me. It's hard to trust someone when you think that they aren't being forthright with you."

Claire looked at Chris. "I understand."

"And while I was mad, I was also scared. I didn't want us to be like my brother and his ex. Arguing over money was just a symptom of something deeper."

Claire responded, "I can see that. And I am sorry."

"You don't need to apologize any more," said Chris. "I've already forgiven you. But next time we start arguing about money, let's ask if there is something else going on. I bet we'll find it to be true."

Claire smiled, "You know, this was not at all what I imagined when I thought about our first week of marriage." She paused. "But I wouldn't change any of it. I think the place and the people we've met have been really good for us."

"Without question," said Chris. "I will miss the resort. But I feel like we're leaving with a new mission to pursue. I feel like we have a better, more meaningful, direction for our marriage and our money."

"We can make a difference in this world," said Claire.

"We can," agreed Chris. "Whether we have a lot of money or a little bit of money, God will use our generosity. We just need to be willing."

"Chris, I really am sorry about not telling you," said Claire.

"Stop it, Claire," responded Chris. "We're moving forward with our marriage and our money."

They both smiled.

Liar, Liar

You open a credit card without your teammate's knowledge.

You keep a private, separate checking account.

You hide a purchase from your teammate.

Trust can take years to build but just a few seconds to destroy.

You probably know the feeling of broken trust all too well. Most of us do. The fallout probably had a dramatic impact on your relationship with that person.

You were confused and hurt.

The Bible warns us about lacking integrity.

> The one who lives with integrity lives securely,
> but whoever perverts his ways will be found out.
> (Prov. 10:9)

> Lying lips are detestable to the LORD,
> but faithful people are his delight. (Prov. 12:22)

> Do not lie to one another, since you have put off the old
> self with its practices. (Col. 3:9)

If ever there is a relationship where trust should be present, it is marriage. Unfortunately, this is not always the case. Remember, the story of my clients at the bank, where the husband maintained a secret credit card account? Research has revealed that many more people out there are doing the same thing.

It is a disheartening thought.

But you are going to be different. You are determined to have a marriage that is the epitome of integrity.

Distrust can quickly divide a marriage. So you are going to do something about it.

How to Build Trust

Trust Builder I: Provide an All-Access Pass

Earlier in the book, I discussed the importance of having joint accounts. I cannot stress the importance of this enough. Joint accounts are awesome trust builders.

I get concerned when I hear about a husband or a wife not wanting to give their spouse access to their account. This signals that something may be wrong. Maybe the husband or wife doesn't trust their spouse with money. Or, like my client, maybe they are hiding something. I have heard many newlywed couples say that they are keeping their accounts separate while they see how the marriage goes. Talk about a tough way to launch a marriage—"Maybe until death do us part, depending on how the first few years go."

I can really feel the love . . .

Even if the motives are good, the upside of providing your teammate all-access passes to all accounts is too great to ignore—communicating transparency, unity, and commitment.

And that makes an all-access pass more than worth it.

Trust Builder 2: Keep Your Word

> "But let your 'yes' mean 'yes,' and your 'no' mean 'no.'
> Anything more than this is from the evil one." (Matt. 5:37)

Jesus was telling us that when we say we will do something, we should do it. This sounds simple enough, but you and I know that following this is anything but easy.

Sometimes, we overcommit. We say yes when we should say no. Sometimes, we forget. Sometimes, we justify breaking our promises, not thinking that it will be a big deal.

But breaking promises is a big deal. First, because the Bible identifies it as wrong. Second, because of its impact on others. Not keeping your word makes the other person feel unimportant, disrespected, and disappointed. Over time, the person learns to simply not trust you.

However, the reverse occurs when we keep our word. The person feels important and respected. They feel like they can trust you.

Trust Builder 3: Be Truthful, Even When It Hurts

Thou shalt not bear false witness against thy neighbor.

The first time I read the ninth commandment was in a King James Version Bible. If the Old English confuses you, it means *don't lie.*

If you have ever been immersed in a context where the people around you do not speak the language you speak, you know that, over time, you get more comfortable with the words you hear. The initial shock wears off. And eventually, you may even begin to use the words they use and speak the language they speak.

In John 8:44, we learn that Satan's native language is lying. When he speaks, he speaks words of distortion.

It's scary when we get comfortable with lying. It's scary because this means that we have been immersing ourselves in the ways of Satan, and we have begun to pick up the language. And the words he chooses to use are intent on destroying you and your marriage.

But the good news is, while lies will certainly create division, truth will unite.

Remaining truthful, even with the small things, builds trust. There will be times when being truthful will not feel comfortable or convenient. These are the perfect moments to build trust. When your teammate says, "You know you really didn't have to tell me that," you have accomplished something significant. Those moments are the moments that build trust.

When you show that you can be trusted with the little things, your teammate will trust you with the big things.

Trust Builder 4: Say, "I'm Sorry"

Guess what? You aren't perfect. You will mess up. You will make a mistake. It isn't a matter of *if* but *when*.

So when you mess up, the best thing you can do is admit your mistake and ask for forgiveness.

Asking your teammate for forgiveness requires humility. Saying "I'm sorry" admits wrong, and that admission is sometimes tough to do. But though you may feel weak, the act of an apology creates strength in the marriage.

Apologies are powerful.

They are acts of love. They communicate to your teammate that they deserve respect instead of disrespect, honesty instead of lies, trust instead of distrust. Apologies point their finger at the wrongful act and say, "You don't deserve that."

And that builds trust.

Trust Builder 5: Forgive

God tells us to forgive one another.

And be kind and compassionate to one another, for-
giving one another, just as God also forgave you in Christ.
(Eph. 4:32)

Just like you, your teammate will mess up. They will make a purchase without considering you and your opinion about it. They will
be selfish. They won't communicate well with you. And it will hurt.

Forgiveness does not mean you forget about it. Forgiveness does
not mean you let them off the hook, that they are not accountable for
their decision. And forgiveness does not mean that the breach of trust
is immediately repaired. Depending on the wrong, trust might not be
fully repaired for some time.

Forgiveness does mean letting go of the resentment and trusting
God with the matter. As followers of Jesus, this is what forgiveness
looks like.

Forgiveness in marriage builds trust. It communicates that you
aren't their enemy, that you aren't standing against them. Forgiveness
can also reaffirm commitment, that even though you are not happy
with the wrong, you still stand by their side.

Forgiveness is not always easy. In fact, sometimes it can be a real
struggle. But it can develop a greater sense of trust between you and
your teammate.

Destroy the Marriage Divider

Don't let distrust creep into your marriage. It will create a chasm
between you and your teammate. Make sure both of you have access
to all accounts. Keep your word. Be truthful. Apologize when you are
wrong. And forgive your teammate when they are wrong.

These trust builders will help you keep suspicion at bay. Be a
couple that trusts one another.

Your Marriage Challenges

Day 27 Marriage Challenge: *Have a conversation about trust.*
Use these conversation starters:

1. What does trust mean to you?

2. When was a time someone broke your trust?

3. What is the best way to communicate trust in our finances?

Day 28 Marriage Challenge: *Create a clean slate.* Be truthful.
If there is anything you are holding back about accounts or
money habits, now is the time to share it. Say, "I'm sorry." And
if your teammate asks for forgiveness, forgive.

CHAPTER 16

Marriage Divider 4—Unrealistic Expectations

The next morning Chris and Claire stopped by the front desk to turn in their room keys. It was a bittersweet morning for them. The stay had certainly been memorable, but they were sad to leave.

"Back to Charlotte," said Chris as he placed the keys on the desk.

"Do you need me to contact the airport shuttle for you?" asked the lady at the desk.

"Yes, please," answered Claire. She let out a long sigh. "I hope this place does alright without Mr. Gunther."

"I am sure they will be fine," said Chris.

While they were hanging out in the lobby, waiting for their shuttle, they saw Terry and Mary jogging toward them.

"Good! You haven't left yet," said Terry. "We wanted to say good-bye before you guys went back to Charlotte."

"Great timing," said Chris, "The shuttle should be here at any moment."

"It was so good spending time with you both," Mary said as she gave Claire a hug. "We will miss you. Have a good trip back home."

"We will," said Chris.

The airport shuttle pulled up to the door, and the driver stepped out.

"Shuttle for Chris and Claire!" shouted the driver.

"Well, that's us," said Chris. "It's been a good week. We'll be sure to stay in touch."

Chris shook Terry's hand and gave Mary a hug.

"Be sure to let us know if you're ever in the Chicago area," said Terry.

"We will!" said Claire as she waved.

Chris took one last deep breath of the salty air, and the newlywed couple made their way toward the shuttle. The driver picked up their luggage and placed it in the back.

Chris and Claire were about to step in the shuttle, when they heard someone yell, "Wait! Chris and Claire! Wait!"

Surprised, Chris and Claire turned around quickly. It was the man in the suit, Mr. Gunther's friend. He was running toward them.

Unsure what was going on, Chris and Claire stood still.

The man caught up to them, somewhat out of breath. "Wait." He tried to catch his breath. "You can't leave."

Confused, Chris responded, "Well, we have to. Our plane takes off in a couple of hours."

The man spoke, "No, you can't."

Chris quickly responded, "Why?"

The man took some papers out from a folder he had with him.

"My name is Ronald Bailey. I was Mr. Gunther's attorney. Mr. Gunther called me in for a meeting the other day. For a while, I had been pushing him to make a decision about the future of the resort should he pass. In that meeting, Mr. Gunther let me know that he had finally figured it out."

Claire let out a slow, "Annnnd?"

"And you are the future," said Ronald.

"Excuse me?" Claire responded.

Ronald explained, "Mr. Gunther saw something in you guys that he had been waiting for. And he felt like you were the ones to carry The Miami Palms Resort and Spa into the next generation. He had me write up the legal documents. See?"

The attorney showed Chris and Claire the papers. Sure enough, it named them as the heirs to the resort.

"But what about Terry and Mary?" questioned Chris. "Why not them?"

Terry stepped in. "Mr. Gunther actually asked us about this a couple of years ago. We have a good life in Chicago. We have a mission there. Our hearts are in Chicago, not Miami. I think you all will be perfect."

Chris looked at the documents again. Then he looked at Claire. This was crazy. This was absolutely insane.

Claire put her hand on Chris's back. Chris was silent.

Slightly louder than a whisper, Claire said, "Honey, what do you want to do?"

The Power of Expectations

Juliet Schor, a professor at Boston College who studies consumerism, wrote these words about our culture: "We went from keeping up with the Joneses, to keeping up with the Gateses."[1]

Our money expectations are out of control. No longer are we comparing ourselves to those in our own economic bracket; we are comparing ourselves to those well beyond our current financial standing. The fallout from unrealistic money expectations is hurting our finances and our marriages.

Expectations are powerful. Managed well, they can motivate us to go further than we ever thought possible. Managed poorly, they can disappoint us more than we ever thought possible.

Have you ever been disappointed?

Sure. We all have.

What led to your disappointment? More than likely, you hoped for or expected something that never happened.

Your greatest disappointments resulted from your greatest hopes that were never realized. The more emotionally invested we are in a desired outcome, the greater the pain we experience when it doesn't happen.

In an attempt to reduce the pain of unmet expectations, we become cynical, settling into the probability of a disappointing outcome.

"She'll probably turn me down for a date."

"I probably won't get the job."

"My favorite sports team probably won't win."

Unmet expectations hurt.

They hurt individuals and they hurt couples. Frustration and resentment can flow from the hurt. Unmet expectations can make your teammate feel like a failure. Worse, they can cause you to mentally mark your teammate as a failure. The pain of these unmet expectations drives couples into venomous arguments. Unmet expectations can create division in many areas of a marriage, including money.

This is why avoiding unrealistic money expectations are so crucial.

Where Do Unrealistic Money Expectations Come From?

None of us intentionally sets our hearts on unreasonable goals. But somehow, we convince ourselves that what is unreasonable is actually reasonable. As it relates to our finances, we can find ourselves expecting to one day drive a certain car, live in an amazing house, take exotic vacations, and enjoy luxuries that are currently unattainable.

We think these things are within our reach.

But for some of us, these expectations just don't make sense, especially in the near future. They are completely disconnected from reality.

How did we arrive at such unrealistic expectations?

Your Background Got You Here

Earlier in the book, we considered the importance of understanding your teammate's story. You and your teammate's background with money will show up in both of your financial expectations. This does not mean that those who grew up with great wealth will necessarily expect great wealth. More important than their family's bank account balance were the money lessons learned along the way.

A Misunderstanding of Reality Got You Here

The misunderstanding of reality causes us to chase a façade, something that is not real.

Media warps our understanding of reality.

I bet you filter the images and status updates you post on social media. If you are like most, you place images and status updates that portray a partial truth of your life. You don't place pictures of you and your teammate fighting or struggling to pay bills.

Neither does anybody else. You are not alone. You present to the world a filtered image of yourself, and they give you a filtered image of themselves in return. But over time, you begin to believe that their filtered image is their reality. You see their house and their vacation destinations and think, *They look so happy. I want that.*

We forget that a large portion of Americans pay for their lifestyle with debt. We forget that 60 percent of people do not have even $500 saved for an emergency. We forget that most are not preparing to retire well. We just think, *They look so happy. I want that.*

Or what about home improvement shows? You look at the house on the television and then look around at your house. Suddenly, you think that everyone's house looks like that. And your house doesn't compare. Their house looks so fresh, modern, and clean. Your house looks dated. The house you once loved is now just one big disappointment. You wish Chip and Joanna would stop by to help. They're just so easy to like.

Look, many of us simply believe a lie, and we need to see through it. We need not always accept things as they are presented to us but know that behind every social media post and every person who renovates their house on television is a real person with an imperfect life. Just like you.

"I" Got You Here

One of the things I have noticed about unrealistic money expectations that result in divisive arguments is that the expectations are rarely focused on others. Rarely do I hear, "I'm angry at you because I want this to happen so badly for you."

No, most of the time there is fallout because someone did not get something they wanted for themselves.

The Antidotes for Unrealistic Money Expectations

So how do we combat these unrealistic money expectations that can divide our marriages?

It starts by being grateful for what you have been given. Remember, God is the Provider of all things. He is the Master in the parable of the talents. You are not entitled to anything. And once someone realizes they are entitled to nothing, they become grateful for everything. So be thankful for what you have been given.

Next, focus on reality. Throughout this book, I've given you quite a few statistics that reflect our nation's personal financial health. The numbers are not encouraging. Realize that many of the lifestyles you see are supported by debt, and it will catch up with them. Focus on reality and don't get swayed by the façade.

Then, spend some time with those who have less. In the parable of the talents, we see that some are given more than others. This means that there will always be somebody with more than you. It also means that there will always be somebody with less than you. So spend some time with those who have less. Not only will your expectations adjust, but you will find opportunities to advance God's mission through generosity.

Finally, place your expectations on God instead money, which cannot be trusted. Place your hope on the One who will never let you down. Concentrate on his promises for you, knowing that he will make good on every single one.

Set Appropriate Money Expectations

So how do you and your teammate set appropriate money expectations? Consider these tips:

- **Become an outsider.** Imagine that you were not you but a friend of yours. And you heard your money expectations. As your friend, how would you respond? Do the expectations seem reasonable? Or are they a little misguided and potentially harmful to your marriage? Are they focused on you or on others?

- **Talk about your money expectations with your teammate.** Remaining silent about money expectations almost guarantees a future blowup because your teammate has no clue that such an expectation even exists. Don't assume that they think like you. As with any money decision or goal, you have to be on the same page. So talk about it. Listen to their feedback. Your teammate may help you turn an unrealistic expectation into a realistic one.

- **Consider your teammate's money expectations.** They will probably be different from yours. Try to understand what they hope to accomplish, and see how you can move forward together as one.

- **Pray.** Sometimes, money expectations run deep. And they can be difficult to adjust. Pray that God will help you develop reasonable expectations. Pray that God will replace your expectations with his expectations.

Destroy the Marriage Divider

Don't let unrealistic money expectations result in frustration and resentment toward your spouse. Don't let them hold you captive, making you bitter about your teammate and your life. Money expectations are your creation. Which means you can also adjust or get rid of them. Put your marriage first. Develop realistic money expectations with your teammate and walk toward them together, hand in hand.

Your Marriage Challenges

Day 29 Marriage Challenge: *Talk about expectations.* Use these conversation starters:

1. How does your money background influence your expectations?

2. How does media influence your expectations?

3. How can you overcome unrealistic expectations?

Day 30 Marriage Challenge: *Commit to living generously with all that God has given you.* Live out the satisfying, adventurous life that God designed for you and your teammate.

CONCLUSION

Rich

It had been slightly over a year since Mr. Gunther passed, and Miami was showing off again. The sun was bright. The sky was blue. The water glistened as it made its arrival onto the shore.

The entrance to The Miami Palms Resort and Spa was as busy as ever. Cars and shuttles were moving in and out of the area, dropping the guests off.

One of the cars dropped off a familiar couple. The staff recognized them immediately. They grabbed the couple's bags and took them off to their room.

A staff member welcomed the couple. "The seventh floor suite is ready for you. Here are your two keys. No need to stop at the front desk. You've already been checked in. It is so good to see you again here, sir and ma'am."

Terry took the keys and handed one to Mary. Then Terry breathed in the salty air.

"Ah, it's good to be back," Terry said.

Mary smiled. "Yes, it is."

Then they heard a familiar voice. "Welcome to The Miami Palms Resort and Spa. It is so good to have you here, Mr. Terry and Mrs. Mary."

Terry and Mary smiled.

"Taking on the greeting role, I see," said Mary. "Mr. Gunther would be proud."

Terry reached out and shook Chris's hand. Mary gave him a hug.

"It's so good to see you again. How's Claire?" asked Mary.

"You can ask her yourself," Chris said as he pointed at the front desk.

Terry and Mary looked to see Claire working with a resort guest. When Claire glanced up, she saw them both and started waving.

"Welcome!" she yelled.

"Go ahead and get settled," said Chris. "I'll check up on you guys later. After all, you are the rich couple."

"Sounds great!" said Terry. He and Mary went to their suite.

Chris looked back at his wife and smiled. It was going to be a good day at The Miami Palms Resort and Spa.

Notes

Chapter 1

1. "Stress in America: The State of Our Nation," *American Psychological Association*, November 2017, accessed March 7, 2018, www.apa.org/news/press/releases/stress/2017/state-nation.pdf.

2. Erica Sandberg, "How Financial Troubles Can Help Relationships: For Some Couples, Economic Emergencies Actually Strengthened Their Bond," CreditCards.com, October 6, 2011, accessed March 7, 2018, www.creditcards.com/credit-card-news/financial-troubles-help-strain-relationships-1266.php.

3. Paul Golden, "Two in Five Americans Confess to Financial Infidelity against Their Partner," *National Endowment for Financial Education*, February 11, 2016, accessed March 7, 2018, www.nefe.org/Press-Room/News/Americans-Confess-to-Financial-Infidelity.

4. Kelley Holland, "Fighting with Your Spouse? It's Probably about This," CNBC, February 4, 2015, accessed March 7, 2018, www.cnbc.com/2015/02/04/money-is-the-leading-cause-of-stress-in-relationships.html.

Chapter 3

1. "Only 1 in 3 Millennials Are Investing in the Stock Market," Bankrate, July 6, 2016, accessed March 7, 2018, www.bankrate.com/pdfs/pr/20160706-July-Money-Pulse.pdf.

Chapter 5

1. Randy Alcorn, *The Treasure Principle: Discovering the Secret of Joyful Giving* (Colorado Springs: Multnomah Books, 2001).

Chapter 6

1. Kathryn Vasel, "6 in 10 Americans Don't Have $500 in Savings," CNN: Money, January 12, 2017, accessed March 7, 2018, www.money.cnn.com/2017/01/12/pf/americans-lack-of-savings/index.html.

Chapter 8

1. Erin El Issa, "2017 American Household Credit Card Debt Study," NerdWallet, 2017, accessed March 7, 2018, www.nerdwallet.com/blog/average-credit-card-debt-household.

2. "Average New-Car Prices Rise Nearly 2 Percent Year-Over-Year, Set New Record High, According to Kelley Blue Book." Cision: PR Newswire, December 1, 2017, accessed March 7, 2018, https://mediaroom.kbb.com/average-new-car-prices-rise-nearly-2-percent-year-over-year-new-record-high-according-to-kelley-blue-book

3. Meg Stefanac, "Car Depreciation: How Much Have You Lost?" *Trusted Choice: Independent Insurance Agents*, 14 Feb. 2014, www.trustedchoice.com/insurance-articles/wheels-wings-motors/car-depreciation/.

Chapter 9

1. David Goldman, "Worst Year for Jobs since '45: Annual Loss Biggest since End of World War II. Unemployment Rate Rises to 7.2%." CNN: Money, January 9, 2009, accessed March 7, 2018, www.money.cnn.com/2009/01/09/news/economy/jobs_december.

Chapter 11

1. "Comparing San Francisco, CA vs. Birmingham, AL." Sperling's Best Places, accessed November 1, 2017, www.bestplaces.net/compare-cities/san_francisco_ca/birmingham_al/costofliving.

Chapter 12

1. I heard J. D. Greear say this in a sermon.

Chapter 14

1. Megan Garber, "How Many Stars Are There in the Sky?" *The Atlantic*, November 19, 2013, accessed March 8, 2018, www.theatlantic.com/technology/archive/2013/11/how-many-stars-are-there-in-the-sky/281641.

Chapter 16

1. Jo Littler and Juliet Schor, "Tackling Turbo Consumption: An Interview with Juliet Schor." *Soundings*, vol. 34 (2006), 46, accessed March 8, 2018, www.hettingern.people.cofc.edu/Nature_Technology_and_Society_Spring_2013/Schor_Tackling_Turbo_Consumption.pdf.